SETTI
INTENTION

11 BRIEF LESSONS ON ACHIEVING YOUR GREATER GOOD

BY

ADAM TAUBENFLIGEL

Love Makes A Man Books

lovemakesaman.com

First edition published in 2021

@adamtriarchy

Printed in the United States of America

Book design by Saqib Arshad

I would not have been able to write this book without the people in my life who continuously reflected back to me my positive and negative sides, until the light won.

My magnificent birth family, my supportive and grounding and hilarious chosen family, my dog Frenchie, who watched me write this book, and Sabrina.

Edited by Jasmin Naim, who came to this book by no coincidence.

I couldn't have found you until I found me.

TABLE OF CONTENTS

PREFACE

I wrote this book because learning the lessons within these pages is what finally allowed me to be the boss of my own life. Once I had felt the success of knowing that no one is in control of me except me, and then using that filter across a range of life experiences, I not only understood that the opportunities in this life were endless, but also how to make them a reality. This way of life and the feelings that accompany it replaced my vices one by one and set me on a continuing path towards the life I have always dreamed of.

I believe that one should take what works for them, and leave the rest, and so with that in mind, I put these lessons into one easily accessible place for others to apply to their lives when the time is right for them to do so.

X - Adam

It was only halfway through July when I finished reading a book I had anticipated would last me the whole fortnight I was staying with friends on the East Coast, but having finished it after only one week, I ventured to the nearby town to peruse the local bookstore for my next adventure.

A few titles caught my eye as I browsed, and I had learned that the town I was in featured in *Moby Dick*, which I felt would be interesting to read while there, but I was really just after a light and easy beach read. My eyes eventually landed on a handsomely decorated little volume titled *Seven Brief Lessons on Psychics*. Fantastic, I thought to myself, I love the supernatural, so a brief foray into this subject matter was exactly what I was after for the next few days. I bought the book and exited the delightful Sag Harbor Books, on route to pack a picnic and head to the beach.

I rode my bike, new book and picnic in tow, to the beach where I set up my spot for the next few hours, unrolled my towel, placed my food down and reached for my new book.

I re-read the title with anticipation, however, this time around noticed that the book was in fact called *Seven Brief Lessons on Physics*. NOT *Psychics*. I instinctively looked up to the heavens and thought, 'nicely done, Universe.'

Physics is not a subject I would ever voluntarily delve into. I remember my brother reading *A Brief History of Time* and trying to explain it to me as my eyes glazed over. That's not to say I wasn't interested but it was just too much information.

I opened the book and was taken by how brief it really was. Each chapter was no more than ten pages or so, and on such complex subjects as quantum mechanics and black holes. Ok, well, let's learn about physics. And off I read.

I was struck by how informative and respectful of time this author was when dealing with things like the subject of time itself, and I finished the book thinking how wonderful to be able to get across such valuable lessons in such an easy-to-understand and direct format.

Over the years I had implemented various practices that have changed my life for the better, but I never knew how to concisely share these things with others. When friends would ask how I'd accomplished one life hack or another, and I told them, I would often hear in response, 'you should write that down.'

So, I began writing them down, in the way that had inspired me to do so via my brief physics lessons on the beach that day, with the goal that the reader would glean the maximum amount of knowledge within the minimum number of pages. I thought, if I can get all of these points down in one central and easy-to-refer-to place then there's no reason why these lessons can't be shared.

If I can learn about physics on the beach I thought, I can write this book, and so, here we are.

INTRODUCTION
THE BASE OF THE PYRAMID

Imagine a Pyramid.

A great Pyramid standing in the middle of the desert. Now populate the town around its base. This is where you live, and life is great here. There is fertile land and a river, and fabulous exotic markets where you can buy and sell whatever your ego desires. As you settle into day-to-day existence in this town your life begins to take shape. The sun rises and the sun sets, you wake up and you go to sleep, but after a while, when the sun is blocked out by the Pyramid, some of us look up and wonder what the view would be like from up there. Most of us, however, are quickly distracted again and forget about that thought, continuing our day-to-day lives. You have obligations to fulfill, places to go, people to see, things to buy and things to sell. Love to fall into, love to fall out of, reflections to look at and reflections to ignore. But after looking up for a while you begin to wonder what happens if we were to go higher? The answer that comes to you in silence is that we see can see farther, longer, clearer, better. A higher perspective in every sense.

This thought stays with you and, one day when the distractions no longer satisfy, you walk to the base of the Pyramid and look for a way up, but you can't find one. You see some other people climbing but they can't hear your cries for advice on how to begin ascending, so you retreat, back to town, back to distractions. You begin to ponder why you can't find a way up, you think to rally a group of people to figure it out, but something tells you that you must go this alone. Something tells you that you can't ascend in groups, as our journeys are inherently ours and ours alone.

You are a bit dumbfounded by your inability to understand why this isn't more straightforward than you think it ought to be, so you sit in silence and continue to think. Moments of silence turn into more moments that turn into full days of contemplation, and in those moments you realize that the instant you set your sights on the top of the Pyramid you already sent your energy there. You're already at the top, now you need to witness the journey unfold.

Beforehand, the distractions of town life felt normal, they were part of how life is supposed to be, but since setting your sights on the top of the Pyramid, you've felt that something isn't quite right with the ways of this human world. The things that used to seemingly fill you up now make you feel emptier and emptier, the more you engage with them. It's as if you've glimpsed into a mirror and you realize that your reflection can see you too. The doorway has been opened thanks to you having quietened your mind and body through silence and contemplation and allowing your gut to guide you to this moment.

'What do all of these worldly activities lack?' you ask your reflection. 'Integrity,' is the whisper back. 'What is this word, integrity?' 'The state of being whole and undivided,' your reflection replies. Knowing full well this reflection is your other half, you know you must reunite your two selves and in this knowledge you can see that integrity will be the cornerstone from which you and your mirror self can begin climbing the Pyramid.

Your reflection winks at you. There's an understanding here that one of you must stay in the physical world, at the base, while the other must begin ascending the Pyramid. Together, with one foot on the ground and one oriented towards the sky, you'll reach all you ever dreamed of.

You walk through the markets, full of exotic wares, unfazed and undistracted by the things that would usually have made you stop. Reaching the base of the Pyramid with a new perspective, you look, as you had many times before, for a way up. As you scan the base of the Pyramid a lone camel approaches, untethered to any human. It approaches you and stops directly in between you and the Pyramid. You think to shoo it away as it's blocking your view and just then, you look into the camel's eye and smile. With that, the camel bends down and you climb onto its back, when the camel stands upright you have just the height you need to pull yourself up, and you do so with ease. The camel begins walking away as your feet disappear over the edge. You wave thanks as you stand up.

You think to yourself, this feels nice, I'm on my way to the top! But before you can celebrate your gains you instantly realize that you're back in the same situation, one level up but with no idea how to keep ascending. That's ok says your reflection, and sitting down, you take in this new view, knowing there is no rush on your personal journey, no competition, no time being recorded. Time, after all, is only a human concept. It is all about you and your reflection, and so you both watch the sunset.

That night, as the stars fill the sky, you sit and think of all the experiences that, and people who, have entered your life that you realize have played their essential roles in your journey to get you to this point. Sometimes you heeded the signs and sometimes you decided to proceed despite their warnings, but no matter, you're here now.

Your eyelids start to become heavy as a warm breeze blows by. A caterpillar crosses your path and you think of it forming its chrysalis in the future. You realize the awesome commitment this tiny creature makes in forming a cocoon because the caterpillar must know it will never be a caterpillar again. Does it know what it will become? Does it know that it will break down completely before being reborn into a butterfly? Doubtful. But it trusts the universe and it goes to sleep, allowing magic to take hold as it does so.

I believe that everything we do in life is done through a certain filter and just as we change water filters, sometimes we need to change our perception filters too. In this book I introduce a different topic in each chapter and question whether, if we viewed the topics with different filters would the outcome of engaging in these behaviors be the same? Would we even want to engage in them at all anymore, if we truly understood that every decision we make alters the course of our lives? Through discipline and patience we eventually learn that breakthroughs are often closer than we think, but too often we abandon our quest just as we're nearing them. Slowing down speeds up the breakthroughs.

Each chapter ends by referring back to our hero's journey (you) and reminding us that simply acknowledging a new way of looking at each topic allows perspective shifts to occur. This clarity lights our path, helping us to continue climbing higher and higher up the Pyramid, until we reach the top.

Earlier, I talked about the co-existence of ourselves and our reflection, because this is the simplest way to convey that, as we age, our reflection becomes obscured to us the more we interact with the 3D world and its plethora of distractions. Our sleeping side, or reflection, patiently waits on the other side, subtly reminding us of our passions and our childlike sense of wonder in little ways, constantly nudging us in a certain direction until, if we give ourselves the space, we have that aha moment. At this point we see the whole reflection and are instantly reminded that it was there all along, waiting to become whole with us again. This is when everything starts to make sense again, but it takes some work to get here, or to get back here, I should say.

Your reflection is you as a child. And so, when you mislead or talk down to yourself, it is as if you are saying these things to your childhood self. Imagine how five-year-old you would react if you called them fat, or stupid, or useless? Every time we do something like this to ourselves our reflection naturally diminishes; it takes a step back as anyone would if they were being treated the way we often treat ourselves. When enough time has passed, we eventually lose sight of the reflection altogether. Self-love brings it back. Because when you tell your five-year-old self you love them, they jump into your arms.

Some people lose sight of their reflections altogether. Others are reminded of them on occasion, and the lucky ones reunite with them after being reminded, and accept who they are and what makes them tick.

The reason I use the Pyramid as metaphor is because I had my aha moment and was reunited with my reflection inside The Great Pyramid of Giza on May 20th, 2019. Arriving at that experience altered my life's course which then shaped the book I was inspired to write on the beach in Sag Harbor that day.

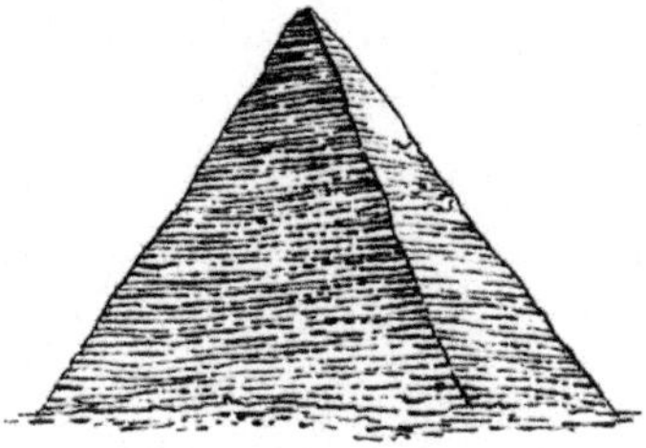

In the spring of 2019 I had to get from Copenhagen to Casablanca and, when I searched for a flight, the first option that came up had a 23-hour layover in Cairo. Normally I would skip any option that had a layover of this length, or at all, but as soon as I saw that Cairo was the stopover, and that I would be there on the night of the full moon, I knew it was more of an instruction than a suggestion. I booked the ticket.

I arrived in Cairo at 5PM and as soon as I switched on my phone, I got an alert from the BBC that an explosive device had just been detonated outside the Egyptian Museum, injuring no one. I thought about it for a moment and quickly realized that giving into the energy of fear would only have confirmed that type of behavior and attract more of that type of experience, so I bought my visa, picked up my bags and set off. Arriving at my hotel at the Giza Plateau just before 8PM, I checked into my room and ate a light dinner on my terrace overlooking The Great Pyramid, with the full moon rising behind it.

I felt like I was on an adventure, and I was, of the *Indiana Jones* kind. I experienced anticipation like a child before a sleep on Christmas Eve. (The truth is that the magic of a Christmas Eve sleep has never left me.) I had a conversation with the moon, as I do every full moon, spoke to my loved ones and went to sleep.

The next morning I rose at dawn and ate breakfast with the same view that I had at dinner the evening before, except the moon had been replaced with the sun, and the sun's heat was unforgiving. No matter, I had on white jeans and a denim shirt. I'm a sustainable denim designer by day and I always dress the part.

I met my guide Ahmed promptly at 8AM and he laid out the day for us, telling me that we would start at Memphis and work our way back, finishing the day at the Pyramids and the Great Sphinx. I objected, and I didn't even know why. I said that, with my limited schedule, I would prefer to start at the Pyramids and work our way out, ending wherever we needed to. I was met with no objections on Ahmed's side and so we set off.

It was a mere three-minute drive to the Giza Plateau which houses the Great, and surrounding, Pyramids as well as the Great Sphinx. We got out of the car, purchased our tickets and walked to the base of The Great Pyramid. That's when everything started coming into focus. I won't dwell on this point too long but if you've been here then you will know that the sheer magnitude of this structure in person is beyond anything you could ever imagine. Photographs and film do it no justice. The Pyramid is a behemoth and it is very hard to believe that it was created manually during a time when rope and grease were some of the greatest technological advances in building methods. But I digress.

Ahmed and I chatted briefly about the subject of pyramids, slavery and extra-terrestrials until he revealed to me that guides were not allowed to enter the Pyramid and so I had to leave his side there and venture in alone. He informed me that I would be in and out in about 25 minutes and that he would be waiting for me outside.

I set off and up the side of the enormous manmade mountain of stone, approached the entryway and entered the ascending passageway. Instantly you are in what feels like the set of the aforementioned ***Indiana Jones*** movie and it is amazing. You find yourself in a twisting corridor of stone, steeped with mystery. I reached the staircase that takes you to the Grand Gallery and this is when my experience changed a bit for the worse. It was busy in here and this staircase is a one-up and one-down kind of ladder, so I had a fair wait while a group of Swedish tourists made their way down. Finally, it was my turn to go up and a few moments later I emerged into the several-story-high Grand Gallery. To say I was in awe would be an understatement. The size and architectural precision of this room are beyond words. Nothing is out of place, and nothing is imperfectly aligned.

As I became more aware of my surroundings, I became aware of how many people were in here, coming up and down, talking loudly, laughing, making jokes, you name it. All I could think to myself was how incredible it would be if everyone would just shut up so we could hear what this structure had to say to us. But that didn't seem like it was in the cards for me, so I slowly made my way up, trying to silence my mind by reveling in all that was around me. I reached the top of the Gallery and had to wait for a group of well-dressed Spaniards to come down before I could climb the last bit. It was clear that I would have to duck to enter the passageway that would allow me entry into the King's Chamber. The passageway was intentionally designed like this to enforce reverence upon entry. Fair enough, as I would soon discover.

After about twelve paces or so more, I emerged into the King's Chamber, straightened myself out and looked at the far wall behind the sarcophagus, which is one gigantic piece of black stone. My jaw dropped. I clutched the side of my head in an attempt to plug my ears to silence the sound or vibration that was entering my head. Did no one else hear this? I realized I must have looked a bit concerning to some of the other guests, and after receiving a couple 'are you ok' enquiring glances, I pushed myself up against the wall by the entryway I had just come through and stood there, getting used to my surroundings.

The vibrations emitted by that wall were so intense that it took me a couple minutes to get my equilibrium back, and when I did, I crossed the Chamber and stood against the opposite wall, as my eyes had begun to uncontrollably water. I wasn't crying, it was a physical reaction to whatever was going on in there. How was no one else experiencing this? I started looking around and took in the group of girls posing behind the sarcophagus in *Walk Like an Egyptian* poses. The

Arab man in a thobe having some sort of argument with his son. A blonde woman walked past me, giving me a look of concern.

The Chamber is 34.4ft X 17.17ft so it's well-sized but not huge. I repositioned myself for a second time against the back wall, farthest from the vibrating wall and the sarcophagus, as I didn't quite have the strength to get nearer to that side of the room. It was there the thought came back to me again, 'why is everyone being so loud?' Why can't everyone be quiet and hear what I'm hearing, and why can't they let me hear more? This became a big theme for me after this day, that in silence we can hear so much, if we just allow ourselves that silence.

I must have been pressed up against the back wall for four-to-five minutes, rigid, penitent, eyes watering, when the man who tends the room, who had been keeping watch by the sarcophagus, made eye contact with me. I gave him a nod, he motioned to enquire whether or not I would like him to take a photo of me as I had seen him do for the *Walk Like an Egyptian* girls moments before? I indicated no, but thank you, and we both resumed our watches.

I kept staring at the wall behind the sarcophagus, trying to make sense of what this Chamber was all about, and what it had been used for, when the same man approached me. He came within about a foot-and-a-half of me and looked directly into my eyes, and then his eyes softened and he nodded and said, 'ah, a good man, wait here.' I did as I was told, which is rare, and I heard him raise his voice to make an announcement that the King's Chamber had to close for a while and that everyone had to leave. Keep in mind that this was morning on a busy tourist day so it's no surprise that I looked around at many disgruntled people as they filtered out of the Chamber, last but not least the Arab man who was the only one wise to the fact that I wasn't moving and he wanted to know why. We made eye contact as he was politely shown the way out and he ducked out of view.

I hadn't put two and two together at this point and so I awaited my next instructions. The man came up to me, took me by the arm and led me to the sarcophagus. He gave me a knowing look, as I asked with my eyes, 'get inside?' He nodded, and with that my heart rate skyrocketed and before I could even think to say yes or no, my leg was up and over the side and then my other leg, and then he was lowering me down and then I was lying down, looking up at him, he put his finger to his mouth and then simply said 'I'll be back for you'. Then he disappeared out of view, and I heard his footsteps leaving my side, out of the Chamber and through the passageway to the other side. Suddenly I realized my wish had been granted. Since I entered the Pyramid all I had asked for was silence so that I could hear. The space inside the Pyramid was now silent, with mine the only body in its center.

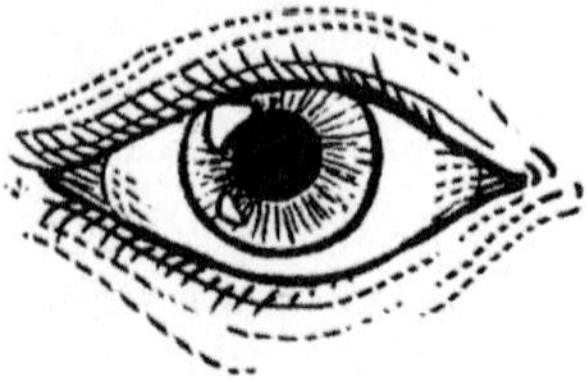

I instinctively crossed my arms over my body and with that I began to shake uncontrollably. My body was convulsing in a way that didn't feel unsafe, simply a continued reaction to my now even more potent surroundings. A few moments of this and I realized that this reaction was also stopping me from hearing the message, so I needed to find a way to quiet my mind and body. I thought of my meditation practice and so closed my eyes and started repeating my mantra with deep breaths. The shaking stopped. With this newfound stillness it suddenly felt as if there were another deeper layer of the sarcophagus, and unknowingly I had just sunk into it.

Then it began. I was seeing with my third eye a lot of blue light, strangely electric blue, otherworldly, but not foreign, or frightening. If anything, I had the comforting thought of going home. Then I saw a little boy who looked a lot like me, on a beach, happy, looking up at me and I down at him. That moment was a second and an hour at the same time. There was no further message to be delivered by this vision because, before I knew it, I was back to blue light and then back to me, lying in the depths of the sarcophagus in the King's Chamber, inside the Great Pyramid of Giza.

I opened my eyes and thought that perhaps I had just seen an image of my potential child, although as the vision settled in the days and weeks that followed, I became aware that it was me I had seen, young unaffected me, my reflection, still there, having a ball, waiting for me to join him. I realized that that little boy, me, is still in me, looking up at me, believing in me, loving me, but was I loving him back? Did I speak to him with affection from day to day or did I talk down to him, call him fat, stupid, useless?

I looked at the hand-carved walls of the sarcophagus and wondered who, besides King Khufu, may have occupied it before me. I would later learn of people, like Napoleon Bonaparte, who had reportedly lain in this exact sarcophagus and had had similarly inexplicable experiences as the one I had just had. For those few moments I lay there with an incredible sense of gratitude for being able to experience this collective energy, and so remained in my gratitude bath until the man returned. I didn't so much hear him come in as just saw his head come back into view over the side. His arm descended to meet mine and he hoisted me up and out.

The second my feet hit the ground I lunged at him with a hug that was the only way of expressing how for the rest of my life I would never forget this experience. He knew what I was saying with that hug and invited me to come back again, and with that he raised his finger to his mouth.

I continued thanking him as I backed out of the Chamber, gave one last bow of reverence to the far wall of energy and exited. I ducked down and took the same twelve or so paces to re-emerge into the Grand Gallery, expecting throngs of unhappy faces, patiently waiting to get in, and this is when things got a little weird. The Pyramid was empty. When I had entered it was challenging to take a step without brushing up against someone and the noise was deafening, as you know. Now, nothing. Just me, and the silence. I was in awe. How was this possible to achieve at this time of day at one of the most popular tourist destinations in the world? I descended the Grand Gallery, taking my time as I did so, and, just as I reached the bottom, a young couple emerged at the top of the staircase, reassuring me that I had returned to the same dimension. We all smiled at one another. I let them pass, turned around to take it all in one final time and then noticed a man at the top, sitting by the entrance to the King's Chamber looking down at me. I smiled and went down the staircase, descended the Ascending Passageway and emerged into the blinding light of the Cairo sun.

I took my phone out and sent my sister a message, recanting the experience in an effort both to share it with her and to keep a sharp and accurate record of what had just happened. I sent the video message that, to this day when I watch it again, gives me chills, and saw Ahmed down below where I had left him, waving frantically at me. 'On my way,' I motioned, and climbed down the Pyramid to meet him.

'What happened?' he asked. 'What do you mean?' I replied. 'You were in there for an hour', 'that's not possible I said, I couldn't have been in there for more than 30 minutes.' 'Look at your watch,' and he was correct, it was almost 10AM. I just stood there, confused. Ahmed said to me that it looked like I had so much to say when I got out of the Pyramid. 'I could see your energy from here.' All I told him was that it was incredible. He looked at me and asked one question: 'Did you lie in the sarcophagus?' 'Why are you asking me that?' was my response.

He went on to tell me that he had been conducting tours such as this for about five years now, and only once had one of his clients been in the Great Pyramid for more than half an hour.

That client had told Ahmed that he had lain in the sarcophagus and that when he did so it was as if time slowed down. I understood what he was saying immediately because my blue-light vision of the child on a beach that felt like two minutes clearly had been longer, and I was completely unaware of this. I nodded yes, telling him what had happened. Ahmed leapt for joy and told me that he had promised himself that, if he ever had another client experience time stop from within the Great Pyramid, then he would arrange for an opportunity like this for himself. I told him that he had to do that, and we bonded over the palpable collective energy between us, as we set off to explore more of Ancient Egypt. I told Ahmed that, even if I got straight back on the plane right at that moment and saw nothing else, this would still be the best day of my life so far. All Ahmed asked of me was to share my experience of Egypt with anyone who would listen. To that request, I say that my experience of Egypt was a land full of amazingly hospitable people and undeniably magical experiences.

It's important to say that this moment in Egypt was a long time in the making. The year prior, I had fallen deeply in love and our time together ended almost as quickly as it had begun, however something unbelievable took place because of this. Before this experience, I believe that I had never known what it felt like to trust and love someone unconditionally. Inviting this energy into my life fundamentally changed my vibration and so, when the physical relationship with him ended, I instinctively knew not to fall back into drinking, drugs, casual sex, or mindless spending. The list of things goes on that I would have used to numb the pain of something like this heartbreak before. Instead, I just sat with it. I inhabited the discomfort and the sadness and the continued reflection of myself in him, while weeks turned to months, and I still did not let any negative distractions into my experience. My ego tried to tell me time and time again that feeling the pain of this heartache so intensely was negative, but I now knew better. I knew that it always gets light after the darkest time of night. That the butterfly only emerges after what must be great discomfort within its chrysalis. It was through this change of filter, while dealing with this heartache, that led me on the path to Egypt.

Every little decision we make sets us on a completely different path, and so by telling you this I want to illustrate that, had I broken up with someone I loved and gone out and started casually dating or having sex to fill the void instead of spending that time getting reacquainted with myself and thus falling in love with myself, even if I had made it to Egypt on that same date I would have had a completely different experience there. I wouldn't have heard the message because I wouldn't have been awake to hear it. I would have been more interested in posting to my social media story than feeling the vibrations of a centuries-old wonder of the world.

I wouldn't have created the silence in my life that led me to the Pyramid, in body and in mind.

We may think it is innocent enough to partake in things we know aren't the best for us, but what is the true cost of this? I don't mean what it does to your health or bank account, I mean the cost of missed experiences like mine in Egypt, because even if you're there, you can still miss it.

You know the saying *wherever you go there you are?* It took months of discipline to be able to get clear-headed enough to be guided into the experience I had in Cairo. The decision we all have to make is whether we are willing to put in the work. The good news is that, as soon as we start, the universe hears you loud and clear and the road less traveled opens up, much like how, when someone sets their sights on the top of the Pyramid, their energy will be sent there, lighting the path for them to follow. When we, with integrity, fix our intention on something, our reflection goes there and holds our place. All we have to do is follow the path that our other half lights up for us.

I'll leave you with one last thought on this before we begin...

Discipline is the strongest form of self-love. It is ignoring current pleasures for bigger rewards to come. It's loving yourself enough to give yourself everything you've ever dreamed of.

Greater than imagined.

CHAPTER 1

MINDFULNESS

QUIETING THE MIND
ABUNDANCE VS LACK

We have a hundred, billion neurons in our brains, as many as there are stars in the galaxy, yet for the most part we are unaware of this, as well as the fact that both the stars, and we humans, are made of the very same matter. In essence, we each have a universe in our heads, so don't we owe ourselves the adventure of tapping into our own internal universe?

Any technological device you own, or may covet owning in the future, doesn't hold a candle to the immense potential power stored in your brain.

We've all heard it said that we only use ten percent of these brains of ours, but I truly believe that there are things we can easily do in our day-to-day lives to increase their abilities. I know because I've done them, and the compounding results are breathtaking.

Every decision we make puts us closer or further from our ideal path, but we will always be course correcting and that's ok. The trick is to be aware of this, and of the things you can do to stay on the right track. You have to start somewhere and luckily the easiest place to start is by reacquainting yourself with your brain.

There are certain times in our lives meant for certain things. The only way to figure out what you should be doing at any given time is by quieting the mind, which will then quiet the gut, and the senses. From this place of emptiness you are open to focus on what will steer you in the correct direction for you, at that time.

When we try to force things that are not yet for us or not for us at all, we experience friction and a longer wait before we reach our destinations. We do this due to societal influences, such as perceptions around certain milestones surrounding a person's life, such as following a path of schooling, followed by marriage and starting a family, then those family pressures and social media, amongst other things, which instruct us to force what is not yet right for us.

This is why a lot of the time when we get what we want, we don't want it anymore. It's important to normalize any age for any stage of life in an attempt not to rush to anything prematurely.

Meditation is the cornerstone of mind elevation. What happens when you elevate your mind? You see better, further, and for longer. A higher perspective if you will, and from that place, you can see forever.

There have been many times when I have been working away from home, trying to finish something and feeling the weight of the day pile up on me, yet I push on, keeping myself on track. When I push on, as my ego commands I do, it's a loss for everyone. If I instead stopped and allowed myself to meditate, and tapped into my spirit, not only would I provide that pause for myself, in both body and mind, but 20 minutes later I would have a fresh arsenal of inner strength and knowledge ready for any challenge. In short, I just recharged my brain.

Studies have shown that 20 minutes of mediation equals 3 hours of REM sleep.[1]

Which I have experienced first-hand. I'll be exhausted and out of it, trudging along as I said, then pursue a 20-minute meditation and come out of it feeling like I just woke up first thing in the morning ready to start a new day. It's glorious to experience. So good, in fact that I think the number one question presidential candidates should be asked is whether or not they meditate. Period.

For me, meditation was the first domino that tipped in the never-ending series of positive life changes that led me to sit down and write this book. Breathwork soon followed, which when done correctly allows you to saturate your entire body with oxygen whilst regulating the production and circulation of cell signaling molecules such as nitric oxide, thus untimely performing a hard reset on your nervous system. All of that in 20 minutes or less. Grounding came next, which is the

---

1 https://tm-ireland.org/transcending-much-more-than-relaxation/

simple act of walking barefoot on earth, something we humans don't do nearly enough of in this modern world of ours. Sobriety was a natural next step, along with countless other positive life changes. All voluntary. None had any power over me. In this way, you start to see clearly the meaninglessness of so many things and you can transform. Immediately.

Life changing realizations of the mind can unlock like this in an instant. It doesn't take years of work, it takes just a moment of clarity. The work is in providing yourself moments of silence, like meditation, which provide the clarity to have these realizations. All you have to do, is listen for it, then the path ahead is lit right in front of where you always stood.

In essence, we are like vessels trying to get into port, and every decision we make is a course adjustment which dictates how we get there. Some decisions speed up the process, others slow us down. It's up to us to be the best captains of our own ships so that we can get into port swiftly and safely. How quickly you reach the points on the journey depends on how you maneuver the vessel that is guiding you there.

Before meditation, I didn't know how to gain control of the steering wheel. I was simply operating from impulse to impulse without having plotted a course. Distractions and desires make us believe they will solve our problems when all they do is create feelings of a gnawing absence that we will never truly fill.

When we meditate, we can quickly shut the ego's voice down and get back on course. Imagine the thoughts that constantly bombard our incredible minds. The feelings of lack and inadequacy dumped onto us in unprecedented volume. In the past we sought out imagery in film or magazines, now, although still needing to seek it out, it is accessible to us in a never-ending stream.

We all know the saying that our thoughts create our realities so what are you thinking about? What is influencing your thinking, is it social media or introspection? And are you giving yourself the space to notice this in the first place? When you feed something it grows, so consider your thoughts and what you are growing, are they serving you?

Meditation allows you the ability to take control of your life, to get off autopilot and get the right side of you in the driver's seat.

This paves the way for applying one of the most important things I ever learned.

Abundance vs lack.

We have been programmed to operate from a place of lack. What this means is that we are always striving for something, wanting something. Then when we get it, we switch our gaze to the next thing and the next thing. Telling ourselves that, when we get to that next milestone, when we achieve that next thing, or obtain that next object, we will be satisfied. It's how our society operates. But we miss the cardinal rule here. When we operate out of a place of lack, we will always be in a state of lack. What this means is that we are inviting more experiences like this in, in the attempt to rid ourselves of them. Stick with me here.

Doing the same thing and expecting different results is the crux of humanity. Its why diets fail, why routines don't stick, because they are associated with a negative. I'm doing this to make that negative thing turn into a positive.

We hardly ever approach any change from the positive. For example, tell yourself, 'Right now, exactly as my life is, at this moment, it is perfect.' 'My life is perfect.' Say that again.

'My life is perfect.'

What we normally do is say, 'I'm overweight' or, 'I need a partner'. 'I don't have this so I need that and then I will be great.' All of these affirmations work against the goal. It's a brilliant ego trick to keep you exactly where you are.

When you embrace that your life is perfect as it is now, you are showing yourself and the universe your acceptance of your life and acknowledging the abundance already in your life. Hence, you achieve gratitude. From this place you can add anything you want.

For example:

'I look great and I'm going to start doing cardio.'

'I love myself and I'm going to open myself up to the possibility of a relationship.'

When you fundamentally change the way you open up to your life, you change the outcome. And the first step towards changing your life is to switch from lack to abundance. The clearest way I know how to do this is via simple quiet moments of mindfulness. Whether that is through a meditation practice or simply sitting in gratitude, whatever your preference you just need to turn it on.

Gratitude is an amazing first step to acknowledging abundance in your life. No matter your situation, you can find things to be grateful for. Even simply acknowledging the miracle of your existence, which is anything but simple. When we switch into gratitude mode, we've switched into abundance mode. We thank the universe and the universe thanks us back.

Simply switching what you are saying to yourself from lack to abundance invites abundant experiences that duplicate. Much as your experiences of lack have been duplicating to date. Our brains are wired to notice things that confirm our thoughts, so if our thoughts focus on lack, our experience will be course corrected to match this. The good news is that, if our thoughts focus on abundance, the course will be plotted justly.

Like anything new, it requires repetition and determination. The more you stick with it, the more it comes back around, making it easier every time.

A nice way to practice this is to stop wishing and start thanking. When you're about to blow out your next birthday cake candles if that's something you do, try thanking the universe in place of asking for a wish. It's a really nice way to practice this energy shift.

If you go about your day trying to manifest change from the viewpoint that you lack something, so you want to visualize better into your life, then you are doing so from a place of low vibration and you are misaligned before you have even begun due to the lack perspective. Step into the reality and feel the feelings of having it now, then that vibration will change your path and light the way to manifesting what you are wanting in 3D.

In short, you will never get to where you want to go by acknowledging that you aren't there yet. That will just keep you where you are. Positive, creative visualization raises your vibration and get you closer to your goal. Daydreaming works but only if you believe it will. Any thought becomes part of your reality the second you bring it into play.

After all, all parallel universes exist concurrently and alignment into your perfect universal path is available at any time.

LEVEL ONE

Walking around the first level of the Pyramid you find two things, one is that you can't quite figure out how to get higher up, and the other is that you also can't find the way back down. This is because, once you start on this journey up, the thought of going back down becomes really unappealing and harder and harder to do, as with each level up, you've exited a lower vibration and so now your higher vibration will have a hard time readjusting to the lower one.

You walk along the first level of the Pyramid towards a familiar smell, coming across a pot hanging over a small fire. There is no one in sight, and simply a sign that says 'enjoy'. You remove your boots and pour yourself a cup of coffee and the smell evokes thoughts of faraway lands. You sip it with a full heart. Deep breaths follow.

There is gratitude in this appreciation. For all the hands that planted the crops, that picked the beans, that roasted them, that ground them, that boiled the water. For the water itself used to make it. The coffee is the tool that brings about this acknowledgement, but the act of acknowledgment is all on you. You could easily just sip it and toss the cup aside, continuing to walk around the first level of the Pyramid, scratching your head for a way up, but instead, in your gratitude you sit.

You finish your coffee and sit in meditation, peacefully allowing your body and mind to connect and converse. By this action, they are reset and recharged. After an unknown amount of time you open your eyes and place the cup back and, looking behind the fire, you notice a seemingly misplaced stone, one you could use as a step. You stand, feeling the warmth of the stone under your bare feet and, after a moment, you put on your boots, take a large stride over the fire and step atop the stone, which grants you just enough room to pull yourself up to the next level of the Pyramid. Up you go.

An abundant mindset lights your path up the Pyramid, lack brings you down. In which direction are you going?

CHAPTER 2

SOCIAL MEDIA AND OTHER DISTRACTIONS

Sitting down to write this chapter, I instinctively grabbed my phone and opened Instagram to check on the nothing that ever goes on there. Why are our phones so addictive, and why do we seem to default to a state of coasting, ignoring our potential and distracting ourselves?

Simply logging onto social media has been shown to increase our heart rates by as many as 40BPMs (Beats Per Minute). The body's response to opening the app is to enter fight-or-flight mode, and thus to release cortisol, because social media can provide so much positive or negative stimulation. Our bodies can't help but prepare us for any eventuality.[2]

In short, when we engage with social media, our bodies are in a constant state of stress.[3] Yes, it's only a little spike in cortisol, nothing to be too concerned about if it were once or twice only, but how many times are you opening the app? That constant stream of cortisol can have a very damaging

2 https://www.medicalnewstoday.com/articles/321431#Cortisol-levels-dropped
3 https://www.helpguide.org/articles/mental-health/social-media-and-mental-health.htm#:~:text=The%20negative%20aspects%20of%20social%20media&text=However%2C%20multiple%20studies%20have%20found,about%20your%20life%20or%20appearance

effect on your body as it suppresses your immunity over time.[4] making you more susceptible to illness, weight gain, depression and memory loss amongst other things.

I liken the experience to watching the news. It's meant to provide us with information to protect ourselves with but, more often than not, just bombards us with negativity and panic-inducing stories, thus lowering our immune response over time.[5] Ironically this leaves us wide open to some of the harms reported in the news in an apparent effort to protect us from them.

These things are designed to make us react like this. They possess the qualities of an addictive drug and so need to be approached in the same way.[6]

The problem is that our society doesn't currently shun social media as it does drugs or cigarettes, and so it is acceptable, a part of life, and has the potential soon to be our downfall.

For example, I picked up Instagram after writing that paragraph and saw that my ex's best friend had liked a photo of someone. Just seeing that caused my heart rate to elevate, my temperature to rise and sweat to form on the back of my neck. I don't have a bad relationship with my ex, nor his friend, so what gives here? My body is simply enacting the ancient fight-or-flight response in an attempt to protect me

---

4 https://www.sciencedaily.com/releases/2018/08/180814101418.htm
5 https://www.bbc.com/future/article/20180104-is-social-media-bad-for-you-the-evidence-and-the-unknowns
6 https://www.forbes.com/sites/alicegwalton/2017/06/30/a-run-down-of-social-medias-effects-on-our-mental-health/#5a452b3e2e5a

from danger, but it has its wires crossed regarding what it's supposed to be protecting me from.

What we don't take into account is that the interactions we have on social media, even just looking at it momentarily, are setting us on a completely different course in human existence. It is causing us to make assumptions about others, and ourselves, and it changes the way we interact with people in real time based on what we've seen on their synthetic displays of reality. Remember the ship analogy in Chapter 1? Imagine if every time you interacted with social media you were effectively altering your course. Each button you push gives rise to another course adjustment.

Armed with this information, we at least have a fighting chance of avoiding harm by acknowledging what is happening and making new choices. Even the act of knowing about the pleasure/pain balance and the dopamine deficit states that these platforms create can lessen their impact.

Now of course that's not to say there aren't positives that can come out of social media as well as negatives, but sharing quotes doesn't lead to positive action. Rather it's simulated self-growth and is a trick we love to play on ourselves. If we aren't already on a path of growth, or awake enough to hear a message, then it's just synthetic spirituality, and the benefit will only be delivered if that message managed to wake us up.

Another fascinating fact I love to share is that it has been shown that our brains don't record a memory as strongly if we are capturing the content with our phones[7]. The brain will register that we are doing the recording digitally, so it literally frees up brainpower for something else. The people taking selfies in the Pyramid better hope that their photo stream doesn't become corrupted, otherwise that memory could be gone for good.

So, what's more important, sharing the story for someone else to process, or remembering it for yourself?

Through these examples we see that social media has the power to be highly distracting, to the point of addiction. It achieves this because, at the end of the day, we are all seeking external validation, but the hard truth is the only validation you will ever feel sustained by is the validation you give yourself. Any external sources of validation will always run out, and you will always have to log back in for more. That is how these businesses make money. In other words, you are their product.

Don't feel discouraged. Like I said, these things were designed like this. But if you know how to make digital media work for you, they will be an asset instead of a burden. A tip in making this a reality is to place the icons for your most visited apps deep within a folder on your phone. If you hide the icons and force yourself to take one or two or three steps to get to them, you allow yourself the pause needed to realize that you don't actually want to open them at all. Try it for yourself and you will see that, more often than not, it is the

---

7 https://ideas.ted.com/if-you-really-want-to-remember-a-moment-try-not-to-take-a-photo/)

reaction to the impulse for the dopamine hit that is sending you there. The way you know this to be true is that, once you've moved the icon, notice how often you go to where it used to reside, as if on autopilot, instead hitting whatever icon now resides there. Move the icon and break the habit by giving yourself a moment to reassess before you engage.

In short, put down the digital pacifier.

LEVEL TWO

The second level of the Pyramid feels considerably higher than you thought it would. That feeling of gratitude followed you up and stayed with you, the distance you can now see is farther than you've seen before, the town looks so much bigger from up here. You can see shops and restaurants beckoning you to come back down and interact with them. You notice each and every distraction and, at the same time, you notice that their pull over you has lessened. In this instance the sun catches your eye as it sets over the town and you decide to be captivated by this sight instead. This vision of creative energy that people have gazed upon for thousands of years before you. You follow the setting sun, noticing the thoughts and feelings you have while interacting with this organic light that creates life. You wonder how we forget to marvel at the sight of the sun, and just as you're having this thought it disappears out of view.

You think to yourself that it is fair enough that we came up with these distractions for when nighttime falls, as the awesome light of the sun is no longer visible. Just as soon as you have this thought you feel as though someone has tapped you on the shoulder, you turn to look behind you and you see the moon, shining greater and brighter than you have ever noticed.

You think of yourself and you think of your reflection, the one you glimpsed that set you on this journey and you notice the similarities between you and your reflection and the sun and the moon. Both powerful in their symbiotic relationship on this planet and the life that is on it, the life that is allowing you to have these thoughts. Tonight will be the first of many nights on which, when you look up and see a full moon in the sky, you treat it with great reverence. As the mark of another cycle of light and life, of the magically reflected light of the sun, extending its glow onto earth for all to see until it rises again the next day. The full moon, you will learn, is the greatest entertainment humans have.

You pull a blanket out of your bag and over yourself as the sky comes to life, one star at a time. You think to yourself, how wonderful to be distracted by the moon and the stars. You look up at the highest one and say to yourself, There I am. There we are.

I'm so small yet I'm all of it. And with that, you fall asleep.

Remember, character isn't made by machine and you cannot open the eye of your heart if your mind is distracted.

CHAPTER 3

ENJOYING YOUR OWN COMPANY

WHY MELANCHOLY IS GOOD FOR YOU

Silence is the most powerful dimension of your life. When all is silent, in and around you, you can hear what the universe is trying to tell you, and there is a lot to hear.

I began the outline for this book in the summer of 2019. By the time I got to this chapter it was April 2020 and I was deep in self isolation due to the pandemic. Reading the title of Chapter Three, I laughed. Well, here we are then. My first thought was, 'thank God for my procrastination in writing this because doing so with this new lens that's been thrust upon us all gives me a lot to expand on.' In the spirit of this book, I'll still keep it brief.

At the time of writing I've been alone in my home with my dog for two months, so this has been an amazing time to put into practice what I preach. There have been moments of happiness and sadness whilst being locked away and I've come to view them as equal experiences.

I say this because I understand that feeling empty is the space from which we can add amazing ingredients into our lives. If we are full of obligations and distractions then there is no room left to add anything new, or anything that would be true to ourselves. We are continually sold the message that being full up is the ultimate goal, but think of how it feels to be at a buffet and being too full to eat. In fullness we have no choice, however, in emptiness the choices are endless. From that place we can peruse the buffet and go after exactly what we want.

We underestimate peace and simplicity.

Being alone is pivotal for self-growth and it follows that feeling sad can be a good thing if you acknowledge it as such. A good way to do this is by acknowledging that experiencing sadness is better than feeling nothing because you are too distracted.

We need to embrace a feeling of emptiness so we can begin to refill ourselves with things we have consciously chosen, not things we have been sold to believe will fill us up. In our state of distraction, we continue to fill up on impulse and as a result we can never be satiated. Too often the feelings of melancholy, emptiness and aloneness all lead back to sadness, and all are classified as negative.

The question is, why do we equate being sad with being bad? I used to, and whenever I felt that familiar melancholic wave wash over me I would try to force it away, but now I embrace it as the glorious contrast that exists in my experience. Without the contrast, how would everything else feel?

Contrast is in itself therapeutic and we should be grateful for it, because it provides touchpoints for different levels of human experience. You can't be happy and sad all of the time. That would be the same as the ocean tides never rising or falling. For one, the moon would be left scratching its glorious head wondering what happened to its effect on the earths water's ebb and flow.

Speaking of saltwater, there is no greater energy release and reset than crying. Our bodies have this function for a reason, yet at times we try to push this valuable feature away. When you feel sadness coming on, embrace it, put complementary music on to be assured that you'll feel the full range of feelings, and maybe even like me, have a little cry, or a big cry, let's be honest.

Then when someone asks if you're ok when you're crying, you can smile and say of course I am, crying is amazing. Who doesn't love a good cry after all, because the feeling of that release is undeniable.

This isn't to say that you can't enjoy your own company without being melancholic but, a lot of the time, people shy away from being with themselves for fear it might go there. Notice how I said being **with** themselves instead of being **by** themselves?

We ourselves are the greatest and most consistent source of company we will ever have in this life so it's important that you get to love you. If you feel sad, celebrate it as a symptom of being alive. It's your ego that's trying to trick you into thinking sadness is bad, so you push it away with distractions. If you never sit at ease with it and uncover why you are sad in the first place, you will never allow yourself the chance to work through it.

Keep in mind never to wallow in self-pity. There is an important distinction here. If you find yourself constantly in a state of sadness then it's up to you to rearrange the conversation, raise the vibration and turn sadness into happiness, thus finding a balance between the distraction and owning our feelings. The point is, the more you are able to spend time with yourself, without seeking distraction, and finding out how to truly love yourself, the more you will be able to embrace all types of emotions without labeling them one way or another.

I will talk about vibration in a few chapters and this will all make a lot more sense. In the meantime, know that feeling sadness and embracing it as a positive symptom of life is high vibrational, and it will attract high vibrational experiences in return.

Experiencing sadness by asking 'why me?', on the other hand, is low vibrational and will show the universe that this is the energy you are requesting. To which, as always, the universe will deliver more of what you ask for with your energetic frequency.

—

You'll notice that I don't talk a lot about romantic relationships in this book because men are dead to me. I'm joking, of course. The reason for this is because discussing romantic relationships when you don't have a loving relationship with yourself is a useless conversation to have. In my view, the main reason people encounter relationship problems is because they don't love themselves when they enter a relationship. You need to start with you.

A really great way of putting this into practice before spending countless nights alone at home by choice is to take yourself out and see how you react to this activity. Go for a walk or out to dinner by yourself (without your phone) and just be. Use the time to go inside yourself and own everything you find. Write it all down. Whatever you find is your responsibility to process, and the good news is that there are others out there doing the same. When more of us start behaving like this then it will become a lot easier to find one another, and then we won't have to deal with all the relationship drama because we've started relationships with others on the basis of a healthy and intact relationship with ourselves.

I would always say that I wasn't with anyone because I had not done the work to get to a level where I loved myself enough to properly engage in a relationship with someone else. Then, when I did do this work, I found it very difficult to find someone else who had done the same work on themselves, so every time I did engage with someone it became really clear that I was only really there to fill a void for the other person, as they had not realized that only they could fill it for themselves. This is something I had been guilty of in the past as well. Even if all of this was unclear to them, us being together was a Band-Aid at best, and all Band-Aids have something in common, they all eventually fall off or need to be removed or replaced. So, instead of replacing partners like Band-Aids, it's better to do the solo work and keep loving yourself. Only then will you find someone else who has too, and that level of magic is worth holding out for.

We rarely take into account that the first part of a relationship happens before two people meet. Each person needs to take ownership of themselves first if two people are going to engage fully in a relationship. When two people are in alignment with themselves, and then they meet, in that order, magic happens.

LEVEL THREE

Your eyes open with the rising sun and you look out over the vast landscape and you suddenly feel very alone. Why am I on this journey alone I ask myself, why can't the universe give me someone to share this journey with? I know I've been doing the work, keeping a positive mindset and putting myself out there but I still haven't brought that person in.

As these thoughts fill your mind, as they do most mornings when you wake up on your own, you realize you owe yourself something different today, and so you change the dialogue. Wow, look at this view, and the thanks I have for the eyes I use to see this view. It's not only the view, look at this comfortable and safe place in which I was able to sleep last night. Look at the life adventure I am on!

All of a sudden you don't feel so alone, and the word adventure really sticks with you. You're literally climbing a Pyramid! You bounce up with all the excitement you would normally reserve for your birthday, a feeling you acknowledge is available to you every day. You notice your energy changing, your vibration getting higher, everything feeling better and more possible. You pack your bag and wonder if that coffee is still available a level down but, looking over the edge, you recall that going back is not an option. Good coffee or not.

Instead, you turn your gaze up to notice that the light of the newly risen sun is casting shadows that make visible the crevices in the stone that you couldn't see the night before. You affix your pack to your back and spit into your hands. Carefully inserting your hands and then your feet into the cracks, you slowly and carefully ease up the side until you can grasp the ledge of the next level to pull yourself up.

Upon standing upright you can't help but reflect on your first thoughts of the morning. You wonder, if you hadn't changed your mindset just then, how long would you have walked around that level of the Pyramid? For how long would you have stayed in a low vibration? Would you have let yourself experience a full day in that mode, instead of snapping yourself out of it, not waiting for someone or something to do it for you, and thus changing your entire experience of life? So often we wait for that other person to make it all better for us instead of making it better for ourselves.

It's very possible that someone is on a similar journey as you, climbing up the other side of the Pyramid, learning, in their own good time, these same lessons as you. This reminds you that everything in our lives comes to us in good time.

You think, aha! Why don't I just walk around this level and see if someone is on the other side, but your gut tells you that walking around each level trying to find out would be a waste of your time because your journey upwards would stagnate. You want to engage with people who have experienced their own journey as well, in their own good time, and not those who are only partially through it like you are, as you could potentially only slow one another down by engaging on this lower level, keeping one another here for a long time.

You're noticing how easily you are starting to be able to hear advice like this from your gut, and how you're not experiencing any pushback in accepting it.

It reminds you that we all want to be the best versions of ourselves for when we reach the top of the Pyramid and see who else made it up there, because we know that you can't make it to the top if you haven't done the work. On reaching the top, the company up there will be not only as amazing as you, but ready and willing to engage. You know there are no short-cuts and no rushing, the lessons reveal themselves all in good time.

You realize your adventure is fully underway now, so you fix your gaze up and start looking for another clue that will take you to the next level, appreciative of your own company as you carry on.

Show the universe gratitude for being able to feel sadness and see how that makes melancholic experiences something to cherish.

CHAPTER 4

SEX AND SHOPPING

QUALITY OVER QUANTITY

Have I got your attention? Good. The title brings up a lot and something different for everyone. I didn't pair these things to condemn them or imply that they are inherently wrong. After all, we need sex to procreate and we need to shop to get food and basic amenities to survive, for the most part. But we also know the other sides of these actions and how words like vices and addictions can be easily paired with them.

As a gay man, I have been made very aware of sex no longer being used as an act of human connection more than as an act of validation within my 'community'. In similar ways, within every community the act of consumerism serves as validation, such that shopping and displaying items of alleged wealth are used as a means of displaying one's worth or status, much like a chiseled body is in the gay world.

By now, I think we all already know what I'm about to say, but this chapter is really here to spell out this one universal point.

All of it, the sex, the shopping, and whatever else you want to throw on the pile, is a means of escaping yourself, nothing else, just you. So, the question must be, why the hell would you ever want to escape from yourself?

I've been on a journey for the past year in which I became aware of the old adage that it takes 90 days to break a habit. For this reason, I started applying it to habits that I felt were steering me off my course of seeking the greater good. First, I cut out Instagram for 90 days, then I cut out random sex with strangers and here is what I learned from that experiment.

Sex is the act of two human beings connecting their physical bodies, and is the greatest energy exchange we can ever perform whilst on this planet. It is monumentally sacred yet it can be practiced at varying levels of awareness. What I can't find peace with is how cheap and easily accessible it has become in our modern app-enhanced world. It's one thing to be wary of STIs, but do we ever think of the potency of this energy exchange and how it affects our life's course?

I'm not advocating that, should you catch eyes with someone and chemistry sparks, you must abstain from enjoying one another's bodies, but when it's treated like fast fashion, without even knowing the person's name, then I learned I needed to examine my relationship with myself and my need to seek validation by engaging in sexual acts like this. I also understand that everyone needs to experience life at their own pace with their own experiences but I wished I had given myself this sexual reset a decade ago, and that's why I'm sharing this here. After my 90-day break from this behavior I noticed a correlation in the growth of self-love and self-respect, with a corresponding lack of my desire for meaningless sex. In this way I'm setting myself up for an encounter with another incredible human being that feels like touching the stars.

This requires a course correction. Do you want to stay the course of meaningless flings, or totally remove yourself from the experience, reset, and correct your course? It's easier than you might think.

Shopping equals instant gratification and validation. You love that thing so much, and you crave it so much and then you get it. Then you think, hmmmm, why don't I feel as excited about this anymore? It's not your fault, it's how our egos are wired, and how our world is structured, always making us look for the next, better thing. In fact, we face a huge uphill battle because, if you live in the rich world, everything is available to us at all times. Ego loves this world of plenty, and when ego is less than satisfied by whatever impulse action we're engaging in, it quickly diverts our attention to the next opportunity. If you find your attention flitting from one diversion to the next, it might help to personify this impulse as 'ego' so that you can actively choose how to respond.

It's why a lot of the companies who rely on us to buy their products rely on us doing so on impulse. It's just the way we are wired. Most of us don't even know we have the ability to pause, reflect, and then consciously make a decision. We are in a fog of autopilot most days.

Energy follows attention. See for yourself. Next time you're shopping, in real time or online, and you're about to buy something, put it down, or put it in your cart and walk away, literally. Go to another store, go to the bathroom, grab a coffee, and then go back. It's fascinating to see that, nine times out of ten, you actually don't want it anymore, and if you do, great, then buy it. But this simple act will change your consumption habits because you are acting from a place of control rather than impulse.

We all know that autopilot can put you into bad situations, and the same applies to sex. Think of the app where it's available to you all the time, on demand as it is now. How addictive is that? Enormously. If you're browsing on there, put it down and take care of business yourself. Then revisit the app and see how many of those people you want to invite over. None.

Acting on the impulse again and again just strengthens the bond of instant gratification and keeps you in an endless loop of ultimate displeasure after the brief highs of simulated intimacy pass. There's nothing sexier than turning down casual sex because it's not a priority for you. I promise you that.

It starts to feel amazing not to have any of those temptations around you, or even better, having them around and not caring whether they are there or not.

Any addiction, including substance abuse, allows you to ignore perceived negative surroundings and circumstances instead of working through them, which is why they're so tempting. In other words, they provide an off switch. I'm not talking about psychedelics as there are multiple benefits to those when properly administered but the rest of it is garbage and will eventually, if not suddenly, turn your experiences to garbage too.

When you do away with the impulses, then you can partake in life neutrally, which naturally invites fewer, but qualitatively better, things into your life. These will come from the place of a nicely expressed man or woman, who owns their divinity and seeks out others who do the same.

I run a sustainable fashion brand and my conversations in sustainability have mainly turned towards mindfulness. In the early days I would speak a lot about the facts and figures behind sustainable and non-sustainable clothing and how much water goes into this compared with that, but what I came to realize is that none of that matters if the person you are giving the information to is asleep at the wheel. The truth is that, unless you are a statistician, it's not your job to know facts and figures about sustainability, but it is your job to know yourself and to give yourself sufficient pause to make decisions that will benefit your greater good.

If you were walking down a supermarket aisle and none of the food had any ingredients listed or nutritional information on the packaging, you would likely ask why this was, no? Similarly, whichever way we shop for clothes, we probably don't even think to ask what this or that was made from, where it was made, who made it, or were they paid a living wage? All of this with a purchase that is going on your largest organ, your skin.

The same goes for sexual partners for a lot of us gay men. All we think to ask is whether the other person has an STI, remaining totally unaware of sex being a potent energy exchange with another human, which shouldn't be taken lightly. Imagine asking, 'are you happy?', instead.

The point is that, if we each owned our individual mindfulness and allowed ourselves the time to act based on reflection rather than impulse, we would do away with so much of the behavior and so many of the actions that steer us off course away from our greater good.

This is about big picture thinking versus short-term gratification, and understanding that our society thrives on our responses to our impulses, so make it a game to beat that system with your cool, calm and collected self-control. That's sexy.

Discipline is one of the highest forms of self-love we can gift ourselves. When we apply discipline and are the bosses of our experience, owning that reality and the successes that come with it become empowering. This behavior grows exponentially once we make a habit of it.

What starts to happen when you act like the boss of your own life is that you start to revel in the feeling of owning your own life, instead of being a victim to impulse and needing to escape the accompanying feeling of powerlessness by acting out on more impulses. When this dialogue changes, your course is reset to the most empowering one you can dream of.

LEVEL FOUR

You're walking along your side of the Pyramid, in the hot sun, knowing you're looking for a way up but also knowing that it will present itself to you when the time is right, and not sooner, so you enjoy the journey, heat and all. You see footprints in the blown sand below your feet, the mark of people who came before you, and as you look behind you see your footprints, a path for others to follow.

The footprints you are following lead to an opening in the stone up ahead, covered by long pieces of canvas, blowing in the wind. You approach with caution. It is indeed an aperture, and a cool wind blows out from within. Do you hear voices? You look in and see a narrow staircase going down. What is this, you wonder. A refuge for weary travelers?

You pop your head in and, on impulse, follow the sounds and scents of earthly delights. On taking a few steps down you instantly feel a sense of restriction in your gut, not expansion. You've come to trust this gut reaction as whenever you have listened to it, it has proven it will never steer you wrong.

Once you've begun to follow this path your gut knows that going down is not an option. Even though it's a new staircase, it's still going down. When we climb back down to a level we have surpassed we experience friction, which is simply because our energetic frequency no longer resonates on the lower levels as we are on our way up.

You stop to give yourself pause before impulsively going down the staircase towards sights and sounds unknown. You ask within if you want to proceed. You think maybe it's a good idea, but you know that only yes means yes, maybe always means no.

So, upon this brief reflection you decide that going down this corridor is not on your path and so you turn around to take the few steps back up, but this motion has caused you to lose your footing and you slip backwards, almost falling down the flight of stairs into the unknown.

You instinctively reach up and find your hand grasping one of the pieces of canvas that covered the opening, so you grasp it tightly and pull yourself up. Up and up, you continue to climb with a newfound strength that sees you following the sturdy ancient fabric all the way up, out of the opening. When you reach the rod from which the material hangs, you use it to pull yourself up and you just manage to get one foot on it which allows you to push yourself up and over to the next level of the Pyramid.

You sit for a while, gasping, in the realization that, if you hadn't stuck your head in with curiosity but then turned and slipped, you may not even have thought to use the canvas as a device to pull yourself up with. It appeared tattered and weak, but thanks to you following your gut, and turning when you did, it presented itself in a new light, bringing you ever further on your journey.

Being open to, but saying no to the impulse leaves you with a feeling you aren't used to feeling, and it's a gratification unlike anything you've felt before, it's gratification and its pride and its self-love combined. You're proud of yourself, and in that pride you feel unconditionally loving towards yourself. The top of the Pyramid never looked closer.

When trying to decide on something, remember that maybe always means no, and don't assume that you are missing out on something you would have enjoyed.

Remember to be grateful for what you don't experience.

CHAPTER 5

NO EXPECTATIONS

AND UNCONDITIONAL LOVE

The cause of many of our disappointments in life is that our expectations weren't met, for which we then hold others accountable, as if they are somehow responsible for our experience of life. We then begin to assign levels of love to others based on our needs having been met or not, therefore making the love we give conditional.

Holding someone to something you have created in your head and then being disappointed when that doesn't go the way you want is insane. Yet we all do it. Conditional love is a waste of time and will never offer a complete feeling of love for you or anyone in your life. If you have a hard time understanding what this means, allow me to share this example.

A woman whom I admire greatly and who played a significant role in setting me on my current, and much loved, life path had been married for just over ten years when her husband came to her one day and said that he no longer felt he wanted to be married. There was no other woman, or man, he simply felt his life was calling for him to continue his journey alone. She retreated to give herself pause to think before reacting (something we'll dive into more in Chapter 8, and in that moment, she pondered the vows she had made on her wedding day, to love this man as long as they both should live. These words held the same meaning to her on this day as they had done on her wedding day, and she realized that if she now, all of a sudden, chose to love her husband less because he was expressing needs that didn't include her, then her love would be conditional and therefore hold no value now or ever. She decided to release him from their marriage in love, and they continue, to this day, to be in one another's lives.

Hearing her story for the first time shook me to my core and, I may have not known it at the time, but it planted a seed for me to one day aspire to have her level of composure, grace, maturity and ability to love unconditionally.

She, I thought (and still think), really understands the concept of love.

So much of our experience with others goes from like to dislike, from love to hate, and what this means is that we aren't really engaging with our partners. Instead, we're just using them as tools to fill voids we don't want to fill ourselves, and when that doesn't go the way we want it to, we blame them, instead of ourselves.

We are all experiencing life in our 3D bodies. You, reading this, are doing so in 3D, but when you read that I'm saying hi to you right as you're reading this, I'm doing so in 5D. HI AGAIN!

Did you look up? I'm not up there but I am all around you, as you are all around me, and we are all around one another, at all times. We live in a quantum universe and that topic doubtless requires its own entire book. Suffice to say that everything is possible, including having conversations with people who aren't in the same room with you. Let me explain how this benefits you from the lens of having no expectations and unconditional love.

A lot of the time when we experience conflict, we feel it's necessary to voice this directly with the person we perceive as the source of that conflict. The problem is that we don't know where we are meeting that other person along their journey and more often than not it just becomes egos yelling at one another.

Here's what to do as an experiment in unconditional love and the release of expectations:

- Have the conversation you want to have with the other person in 5D.
- Sit in silence and imagine the conversation.
- Imagine saying everything you need to say and imagine the response you would like to get from a place of love.
- Experience that whole conversation for yourself and see how it neutralizes your 3D desire to bring a lot of these things up.

If you commit to this process, more often than not you will feel an energetic shift surrounding your grievance entirely and you may be able to let the whole thing go. That's unconditionally loving yourself, and others at the same time.

Of course, there are things that have to be said, but in the same way I suggested in Chapter 4 putting something down before proceeding to buy it, try putting down a conversation before you have it, and just have it with yourself instead. You start to realize most of these grievances can be sorted out internally as they are likely more about you and your ego feeling bruised than anything else, and if nothing else it will filter out a lot of what doesn't need to be said at all.

The desire to be right should not be the most important thing. When you've neutralized the energy surrounding a grievance it will empower you to know you are in control of your experience of it.

Now, it's important to remember a few cardinal rules when embarking on this journey. The most important of these is that somebody's behavior towards you is a reflection of their relationship with themselves. Read that again, and again, and again. It is the truest thing you can ever apply to your relationship with others, and once you really let that sink in, it immediately diffuses disappointment, anger and distrust, and replaces them with feelings of unconditional love.

Even in cases of abuse this can be applied, but it is imperative that you physically remove yourself from the situation before trying to put it into practice.

The next most important rule is to remember that, in many of life's experiences, we need to look at disappointment and unmet expectations through the lens of being grateful for what we didn't experience. We get so hung up on things not going the way we had hoped, but we never think of what the universe saved us from experiencing. I have to remind myself to be thankful when something doesn't go the way I wanted it to initially, knowing that the universe is always looking out for me.

When you avoid experiencing whatever the universe has saved you from, it opens up the space to let you focus on your spirit, your reaction, your betterment, and your relationship with yourself. This allows you to approach disappointment and unmet expectations from the perspective of gratitude.

Having a beautiful relationship with yourself will allow you to have a beautiful relationship with others. If everyone applied unconditional love towards themselves, our experience of disappointment in unmet expectations would no longer be.

LEVEL FIVE

You've dusted yourself off from that last spill and you're higher than you've ever been before, both figuratively and literally. You're still beaming with self-love and want to replicate this within yourself again and again, when all of a sudden you see another person!

The person is walking towards you but they haven't seen you yet. What will you say? What will they say? This is exciting, you are in such a good place and you can't wait to share stories about what brought you both here and about how to help one another climb even higher. You knew the universe would deliver someone when the time was right. You stand up. They see you, then stop.

You lock eyes, but they don't return your gaze of excitement. They turn around and begin walking away from you. 'Hey?!' you yell, but they don't stop. You begin moving towards them at a rapid pace. Confused by their reaction and not wanting to lose the chance to speak with another person while on this journey, you swiftly follow.

Your calls go unanswered. You reach them and lightly place your hand on their shoulder. They spin around aggressively, demanding, 'what do you want?' You reply, 'Nothing. Just to talk.' 'Talk to yourself. I'm not interested in talking to you.' And they carry on.

You're left in their dust, and you're confused. How could someone just brush me off in a situation like this when we're the only two people up here? We could have helped one another climb higher. Your ego has a thing or two to say about this and you're about to open your mouth to say the first reactive thing that comes from your larynx.

However, your higher voice has something to say about this as well. It seems the higher you get, the more clearly you are able to hear your true self over your ego, and so you let that true self speak first, before opening your mouth at the request of your ego.

As you watch your mysterious level companion walking away from you, you think to yourself, 'What does their reaction towards me have to do with me, with my journey?' The answer, of course, is nothing.

You are suddenly very much aware of your ability to talk to yourself, as we all are and as we all do, all day every day. We have a choice of which of our voices to engage with and listen to. Ego or gut? 'When does it ever work out to listen to ego?' You think. 'I would have just sworn at that person for brushing me off.' Inciting a yelling match most likely, as their ego was instigating.

You recall how your gut never steers you wrong, so you quickly converse with yourself, and with them in 5D, saying, 'I'm sorry you didn't want to connect with me, but I wish you well on your journey my friend, and I send you love.' You instantly feel lighter, and the desire to lash out has passed. Then something unexpected happens. They stop.

You see, up here, in the higher levels and in 5D, energy is felt by all, so they felt your message of love as a response to their behavior, thus diffusing it for you both.

The mysterious character of your journey returns, and smiles. They clasp their hands in a U shape and stare at you. You stare back. Then they look up and you get it.

Placing your foot in their hands, you are hoisted up to within reach of the next level. You grasp for the edge and fumble yourself up and over. Rolling out of sight for a moment you clamor back to the edge to offer your new friend a hand up, but they are nowhere to be found. It's just you again. You hear a flutter of wings and look up to see a Pharaoh Eagle Owl, flying away from the Pyramid as the sun begins to set on another day.

Again, you feel the inexplicable feeling of self-love, of pride in your reaction, of not making their behavior about you. Of giving yourself the pause in which to hear your higher self over your ego. 'How quickly the path opens up when I behave like this,' you think. 'How quickly I'll reach the top if I don't stray from this path.'

You swing your legs over the side and watch the sun disappear from sight over the horizon, a smile from ear to ear, grateful that it will be back again tomorrow to light your path, and excited that the setting sun means the moon's glow is only moments away, about to light your dreams.

Everyone is in our life for a reason, although not necessarily the reason we want them to be.

CHAPTER 6

EGO

IT *IS* ALL ABOUT YOU(R) EGO

I would like to begin this chapter by saying that my ego and I agree that it should be written (I think).

We can never do away with our ego entirely, so don't worry about this being a chapter on how to kill it. In fact, I want everyone to know that we don't want to kill our egos, we just need to bring them up to date with the times in which we live. It's as if you had bought a computer the year you were born, and had never updated its software until today. Imagine how that computer would run. That's the deal with our egos. You can liken it to an outdated computer program we have inside of us, which most of us live our whole lives without ever upgrading. If we never upgrade the software, we simply can't make the most of the machine.

In this book I'm not speaking of the ego as being the definition of darkness, I'm referring to it as an outdated application of the fight-or-flight mechanism within us. The ego likes to promote procrastination and stops us from starting new projects in an effort to protect us from failure.

Unfortunately, this defense mechanism also hinders any possibility of succeeding as well.

The ego says to you, 'I've got this. I'm going to protect you,' so you watch TV instead of starting that new project or diet or whatever. The intentions are honorable, but they keep you on an infinite loop, going nowhere.

Much like the empowering feeling of being the boss of your life through discipline, you can start to record the feeling of success and accomplishment, little by little, and with that, the realization that you can succeed far outweighs the fear of failure. But it's a tricky loop to get out of.

It's a lot easier to talk about relationships, other people, gossip, all the things that don't get you any further in life because the ego knows how to make you feel better through partaking in these vices, but they're addictive, and negative, and in the end, get you nowhere.

Low self-esteem? Shyness? All ego. We are not inherently shy or think poorly of ourselves but our egos, with their good intentions of protecting us, will have us avoid situations where we might be rejected so we shut in and shut down because our egos perceive that it is safer this way.

Judging others? Making fun of others? Ego. Pushing ourselves up by pushing others down is a completely unsustainable way of trying to prove your worth, and a sure-fire way to prove that you in fact don't love yourself at all.

This is why it is important to remember the lesson from Chapter 5 that people's behavior towards us is a direct result of their relationship with themselves and their egos.

The ego also exists to amplify our beliefs and direct us to pay attention most to what we identify with. So, if we're constantly greeting the day with pessimism and low self-esteem, our egos will continue to direct us into situations that confirm those beliefs so they can be proved right, so you can be right. In this way it's helping you, right? Well, in a way, yes. It's confirming your beliefs. But are you aligned with those beliefs? Do they serve you? What if you change that dialogue and you greet the day with optimism and high self-esteem? Well, then the ego is going to work to confirm those beliefs instead, and will do so in the same way, but this time in a way that makes you feel good, if you let it.

Think of your birthday for example. I don't know about you, but I always wake up on my birthday feeling wonderful. Feeling like no matter what, today is my day and is the best day ever. Someone suggested to me that, in my mind, I could make every day my birthday, so then why can't every day be my day? Why can't I experience this exact feeling all the time? I can, and my ego will help me to do it. I just have to tell it what to do. After all, it's my ego.

There's no point attacking your ego for holding you back. It's just doing what used to work, we're the ones changing the script. Back in the day, your ego would enact flight-or-flight to stop you from walking into a lions' den and thus save your life. Our reactions towards modern-day situations makes the ego think it still needs to save your life instead of just avoiding embarrassment, so thank your ego for looking out for you. Make your ego your friend. Show the ego it can be fun like this. Don't get mad at your ego or judge it for getting in your way. Take your ego's hand and say, 'Hey, let me show you that this new way is ok, let's do this together.' There's really nice energy around approaching it like this.

Perception is everything and, at the end of the day, it is our job to see things right, not set them right.

Ego will want to get involved with everything. But this is not the path of least resistance. Lead by example by releasing the need to keep tabs with anyone. The path of least resistance is non reaction. And this the ego likes least. When you become able to identify the difference between reacting out of ego and reacting out of spirit, that is where the power lies.

When it comes to dealing with other people egos, it's very handy to remember a simple but effective truth. The ego is insane, and trying to make sense of something insane is in itself insane.

This one simple truth has allowed me to avoid so much conflict in my life I cannot count the times. When one ego lashes out to another it can go on forever, swallowing up whole relationships. Don't take the bait.

Resist the urge to respond right away. That is just your bruised ego looking for validation, with its finger on the trigger, giving you bad advice. In silence you are not avoiding, instead you are recognizing which part of you is looking to engage with the situation before you do so, if you do so.

Your silence is your ability to identify that that is your ego wanting to have all of those conversations from a place of reaction. Silence is taking your ego's finger off the trigger and saying, 'thank you for looking out for me but we're not going to look outside of us for an apology or an explanation because that would give our power over to that external thing.' Whenever ego is trying to convince you that your discomfort is due to someone or something else, this is giving your power away to that thing completely. If you do that you will never be able to change what you don't like about it. If you own it, you can change it.

Yes, an apology or explanation may make us feel better in the short term, but words can always change again and again, and we are bound to end up feeling hurt and looking for an apology again if we don't own our own emotions and control them in the first place.

That is spiritual maturity expressed in the real world, which gives you a taste of being the boss of your own life because it proves that no one else controls you. From here, in the present, the possibilities for initiating new loving experiences are endless.

In practice, we can be responsible instead of being a victim. Own your emotions instead of looking for someone else to assuage the pain, because you need to address it yourself. We often think we need to talk in real time, but addressing something directly doesn't necessarily mean having to address it with another person, because more than anything you need to address it with yourself first. Most people miss this step.

An apology is an illusory fix that doesn't remove the trigger, meaning that similar experiences will keep repeating in your life. 'I talked to them, they said sorry, so I feel better', instead of 'I dealt with this, they aren't responsible for my feelings.' An apology is a Band-Aid. If you want to generate permanent change, you will need to acknowledge that cause and effect are both inside of you, which creates the conditions for the wound to heal.

How many times have you thought and thought about what you need to say to someone, when you could have been using that time to say those things to yourself? Take your time on this step. There is no rush, because time is only a concept. What time is good at is buying you grace for when you are ready to engage.

Ego will trick us into thinking, 'see, I talked to them right away and got an apology or an explanation and all is well.' Here I would say, think of a whack-a-mole. Bat down the experience temporarily and it will poke its head up somewhere else. This is why we have so many repeating experiences in our lives. You need to deal with problems at the very root, and those roots are within you. It can be very confusing because we think having external validation will work, but then we're confused when similar experiences keep recurring.

When you approach a situation from this stance, it's not to say that you won't be able to have your voice heard, but when you do, it will come up naturally, without abrasion because it's not coming from egoic reaction. In which case it will be heard in that higher vibration of your energy because you have dealt with it within yourself. This will garner a durable result, at which point, having the conversation or not becomes irrelevant, because you've already dealt with it internally.

You don't need to plan for this happening in the future, because the universe will make it happen when it's meant to, all you need to do is focus on yourself in the here and now. Trust that the only person you should be talking to about anything to do with you, is you, and knowing that it's your ego that wants all the rest.

Now that you know this is the way to achieve bliss, you can administer this antidote to conflict right away. The alternative is to again go through the unnecessary experience of trying to decipher who was right and who was wrong, which is irrelevant when you own the experience of your life and take responsibility for it.

The freedom of understanding that nothing has power over you because everything in your life is your doing is one of the greatest things I have ever learned. You can't be powerful over parts of your experience and not others, much like how a woman can't be just a little bit pregnant. You either are in control of your life or you're not.

The only way to really explain this to others is to be the example, so when you stay in this eternal presence, and lead by example, you'll radiate love, and receive the same in return.

It will feel so counterintuitive to behave like this at first, but when you live it you will know it's the only way. It's a glorious rabbit hole leading to a new dimension you'll create for yourself.

LEVEL SIX

The sun has now set and the moon is high in the sky as you turn around to explore this new level. Upon standing you see an old carpet in a copper bucket tucked up against the side of the wall. You unroll it and lay down to sleep a little, gazing off into the distance, farther than you've ever seen before.

It seems like you are about halfway into this journey when a familiar voice of doubt steps in.

'This is good enough, no? I mean, the rest seems really high. You should stop here.' A familiar feeling of worthlessness washes over you, one you recognize from before, in fact, the same one that stopped you from starting to climb up this Pyramid for so many years in the first place. You are surprised to hear it up here with you now.

Didn't I do away with this, with my ego, always out to sabotage me? You start to feel angry, the same pattern as always with these inner dialogues. The anger is of course low vibrational, and so once you start putting that energy out it starts coming back and can quickly be self-defeating. But you're onto this pattern, and as they say, knowing is half the battle.

So, you lie on your back gazing up at the stars and you say, 'hey, Ego! Look up at those stars with me. Did you know we are made of the same things as those stars?'

You feel calmer, you feel ego's grip loosening. You keep talking.

'You know, Ego, I really appreciate you looking out for me. I know that you have my best interests at heart, and I know you are just trying to protect me, but things have changed.'

'How?'

'Well, before, when humans were first starting out, you would protect me from putting myself into dangerous situations that would have gotten me killed. Nowadays it's really rare that I'll be killed on a day-to-day basis, but whenever I perceive a threat of any kind, you still jump in like you're trying to protect me from getting eaten by a lion, and it really slows us down.'

'Really, no lion threats these days?'

'Nope, and it seems you only feel the signal I give off, you can't see the actual threat, so I wanted to tell you that most of the time when I'm scared it's because of something like fear of failure or losing something, or not getting ahead in life.'

'Those aren't very big deals. I thought I was saving us from getting eaten.'

'At times I was about to be in harm's way, and then you stepped in to stop it from happening, but those times are very rare.'

'Well, you are the vessel that's carrying me, so if you go, I go. I'm just doing my job.'

'I see that now, and I'm sorry I never cleared this up before. I realize that it's my job to update this software, not yours. So now that we know this, can we update your reaction to these new modern-day situations?'

'Of course, I still can't believe none of your fear signals were ever about getting eaten.'

'And I never realized that you can't see the threat, you can only feel the fear signal, so I have to be aware of this. We need to do this together so that we can achieve everything we've ever dreamed of.'

'We?'

'Of course, we. If you're in me, then it's we. I am you and you are me and we're in this thing together for the long haul, so let's figure out how to work like a team and make double time up this Pyramid.'

'I know how.'

'Tell me.'

'Tell yourself how much you love yourself, all the time, because when you're saying that to you, you're saying that to me, and that

lifts both our vibrations. It will remind us that we're made of those stars up there. That energy will keep us in synch.'

'Good idea, Ego, thanks. I will, and I'll also remind us both that everything we do is working towards getting us to our goals, even the setbacks.

Oh, and I love you.'

'I love you too. You know, it's pretty impressive how you've come this far.'

'Well, I couldn't have done it without you. Any idea on how to get up to the next level?'

'Hmmmm, yes. Let's get a good night's sleep and tackle it together in the morning. Rest is important for us and we're not in a hurry. You deserve a good night sleep.'

'We deserve a good night's sleep. Sweet dreams, friend!'

'Dulces sueños.'

You have an amazing sense of contentment for having finally understood the dialogue between you and your ego and that the power to update this relationship was within you the whole time. With this upgrade, you think, anything is possible.

As you close your eyes and fall asleep, you remember a saying you used to hear as child, 'Follow your dreams, they know the way'.

With that last moment of waking consciousness, the carpet you are using as a bed gently lifts off the ground and, under the glow of the moon and the stars that are all made of you, it carries you and your ego up to the next level of the Pyramid, gently laying you down to ensure you both get that good night's sleep.

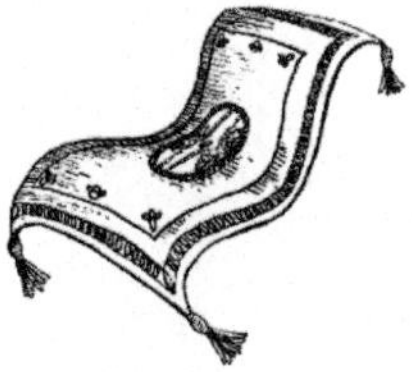

Always replace judgment with compassion and remember that it is our job to see things right, not set them right.

CHAPTER 7

LETTING GO MEANS LETTING FLOW

YOU DO YOU

I feel really strongly about this. Letting go does not mean that you have to remove and distance yourself from people and things, because that actually isn't letting go. That is taking action to force a result. Letting go simply means inaction and neutrality. Letting it be. Neither pushing nor pulling.

If you are holding a rope and you let go of it, your only action is releasing your grip, you aren't releasing your grip and also swatting the rope away. That's not letting go of a rope. So why is letting go of a person or thing often portrayed as a multi-step process?

When we assign negative connotations to something and thereby determine that we must relinquish it, we are assigning the wrong vibration to the thing, thus creating the same repetitious feedback loop in our lives.

Energy attracts energy, so at any given time if you are vibrating negativity over a situation then you are inviting more negativity into your life via that vibration. Your valiant efforts to let go are actually just holding onto the general experience, ensuring that you will experience it again next time around, with the next person or the next thing.

This is why we see so many people repeating patterns with people in their lives. They think, this is bad, so I'm going to let go, and put up a boundary. Then lo and behold, it all happens again with the next person, and the next.

It's also why so many self-help resources thrive, because they teach a method of doing away with all that is bad in your life by affirming yourself positively and the other thing negatively, only reinforcing the negative thing you are trying to do away with.

Much of the time, the concept of creating boundaries is touted as a wonderful way of letting go and putting yourself first. Unfortunately, a boundary is a negative entity. We talk so much about our dislike of nations building walls, yet we jump at the idea of instilling boundaries for ourselves with the people around us. It feels contradictory.

When we show the universe that we are putting up a wall, we are putting up a defense. And when we approach anything from a position of defense, we are inviting more attack.

Letting go does not mean having a conversation and stating your intentions, nor does it mean announcing you are putting up a boundary, it simply implies inaction.

The whole concept of putting up boundaries to protect yourself is a misfire in energetic alignment. Boundaries avoid triggers instead of working through them, and working through them is as simple as believing and knowing that you are in control of the situation and that you are able to change it from a simple place of graceful non reaction.

If your ultimate goal with someone is to instigate a change in their behavior, then do you really think announcing something with a negative connotation is going to create a positive result? This is another outdated ego practice, and we dealt with that in Chapter 6.

The thing is, when we make the announcement, or put up that wall, we feel a sense of righteousness and empowerment because we put ourselves first, but we achieve this by putting something else down, and that's why it doesn't work.

The only way it works is from a place of neutrality. If something isn't working for you, that does not make the other person wrong, it just means it's not working for you. So, you have to let go of needing the satisfaction of being right, you simply need to let it flow.

Remove yourself, without conversations or announcements. Simply, calmly, gracefully and elegantly, remove yourself to whatever level you feel comfortable with. It's not putting up a boundary, it's removing all of them.

This energy will naturally open a door for conversation if a conversation is warranted. If not, there won't be one. Especially if you have that 5D conversation and neutralize the energy yourself, as you know now you always have the power to do.

How many times have you been on the receiving end of someone's conversation about their partner or their ex, and how many times have you been the one speaking? Letting go of someone in the physical sense and then talking about them non-stop to someone else is not letting go, it's holding on with a death grip.

What you resist persists. Talking about it keeps you engaged. It makes you feel proven right. It makes you number one, and it keeps you miserable. In short, it's the opposite of a peaceful flow.

Does a river flow downstream and then stop for a second to talk about how it's going to keep going downstream? No, it just flows. If you let events flow then you are allowing life to lead and allowing it to unfold along your right path.

Therein lies the difference. Letting go, with all its modern-day babble, is the opposite of letting flow with peaceful inaction.

Remember that all the situations that occur in life are impulses from the universe nudging you towards your greatness, so don't demonize anything or anyone. Be constantly grateful for the reflection and contrast these experiences and people are providing as you allow them to flow gracefully in and out of your life.

On the topic of acceptance, it is important to remember that acceptance is not finality. Often, I would feel if I accepted a situation as it was, and if as it was were not how I wanted it to be, then I was in a sense accepting defeat by accepting it as it is. This is not the case. By accepting the situation as it is, you are allowing for the situation to be fluid, and by allowing it to be fluid you are allowing it to move in the direction it is meant to move in. If you resist accepting it then you are not giving it that space to move forward.

When you accept things as they are instead of resisting them, then you are flowing with the energy of it, and allowing yourself to be at peace. This in no way means it's going to be like this forever, but we have to accept in order to keep moving forward, otherwise we keep walking in a circle of non-acceptance, wondering why nothing is working out for us.

I like to call this the acceptance and surrender experiment, in which we flow in collaboration with life, trusting the timing and allowing success to be a byproduct. Don't resist this.

Holding on, or actively trying to let go, fills your present with the past and restricts the freedom of the future, so when we undo the past by letting it all flow in the present, we release our future.

After all, if you want to fly, you have to give up the shit that weighs you down, and that isn't composed of other people or things, it's entirely made of your way of dealing with them.

LEVEL SEVEN

Your eyes open and adjust to the horizon, a horizon that appears slightly different from when you went to sleep the night before. You rub your eyes and look around and count the levels below you, and, peering over the edge, you see the copper bucket from whence you retrieved the carpet the night before. You can't quite tell if you're dreaming or awake but somehow, in your sleep, you made it up another level. Unfortunately, your sack did not, but you know there is no going back and as your water bag is still attached to your belt you know you can make it the rest of the way.

'Teamwork,' you hear your ego say. Indeed, you say to yourself as you eye the carpet beneath you. A magic carpet! But before you even think of asking it to carry you to the top, you know it was only ever going to carry you up to this next level, if that's indeed what happened.

You roll the carpet up with gratitude and carefully, leaning over the ledge, drop it directly into the copper bucket below. As you do so you let the experience of the carpet flow through your life. Not expecting anymore, not holding on, not letting go, just flowing into your next experience.

'Bullseye,' says your ego. You wink, standing up tall, stretching it out and basking in the glory of another day.

You take a sip of water, noticing your increased state of contentment as time goes by, not from having or not having anything or anyone, but because of your neutral existence and how beautiful you appreciate this to be.

But you do wish you had some food. Either way, you look down at the Nile, glistening in the morning sun and you think to yourself that the banks of a river don't complain about the water rising higher or lower or going faster or slower, they just allow the water to flow, and so you remove resistance from your experience and allow life to flow all around you.

With that, you take another sip of water and fix your gaze upwards.

What is meant for you will not pass you by. Have faith and remove the uncertainty from your journey.

CHAPTER 8

REACTIONS

SELF AND OTHERS

Regardless of what happens to you in life, you will always be able to control how you react to any given situation and your reaction creates your reality.

Read that again.

The goal here is to make your reactions beautiful for yourself and those around you. All day we are in situations with ourselves and others that ask for a reaction from us and, more often than not, our reactions come from impulse, not from introspection.

When we really grasp control of this, we are able to take full ownership of our experience of life. For me, this was one of the lessons that stuck with me most and which continues to this day.

It is hard to remember because life is busy, but as with most things in this book, when you start to notice how positive reactions feel, you will start to multiply that experience. I am not only talking about experiences with others. More often than not, I am talking about experiences with ourselves.

For example, on recently making myself my usual morning smoothie, I sat down and opened a magazine to read an article that interested me. Upon reaching for my fresh blueberry smoothie, I knocked it over onto my phone, the table it was resting on, as well as all over my light grey shag rug. In short, it was a disaster.

Now, I have been known in the past to react to situations like this much like how a volcano reacts to a large build-up of magma within its core, but upon applying the concept that I am responsible for my reactions, I understood that, regardless of whether I exploded or took a deep breath, the smoothie would have to be wiped up and I'd have to make another one. So now I always choose the latter response.

To be perfectly honest, the things that jumped into my head when that happened were along the lines of 'wow, you're such a loser, can't you just drink a smoothie and keep it together?' But when I catch myself on that behavior now, I picture saying that to my five-year-old self and I immediately change my dialogue. Instead, I say 'That's ok, I'll clean it up and make you another one, no problem.' I thank the universe for this wonderful experience of contrast in which I can hear these things and experience this action without falling to pieces. Then instantly, I become so grateful for the smoothie spilling because it has shown me how far I've come on my journey of measured reactions.

The next phase, however, can get a bit trickier. That is, managing reactions towards others.

This one requires a lot of practice. It's one thing to get in check with yourself, and a lot easier to do because you aren't reacting to anyone else's energy. It is far more important to get your responses to others in check as this is the one that can really impact your experience of life.

Remember when we talked in Chapter 5 about having 5D conversations with others? That goes a long way when you have the time to do them, but if you are in a real-time conversation with someone, then you are in real time. In which case you have to be on your toes because now you are dealing with someone else, and their ego, which let's face it, probably hasn't been upgraded like yours now has. The problem with you engaging with an unrefined ego is that it makes it a lot easier for your ego to slip into its old programming and the results can be less than ideal.

The fun thing about this is that it can start to feel like a game in which you use your self-mastery to defuse situations before they even begin. What you will notice is, even more amazing, that it starts to rub off on those closest to you and they begin to wonder what this non-reactive way of life is all about, and then everyone's lives start feeling a lot less complicated.

There are a few key methods to easily remember why you should control your reactions towards others.

If their behavior towards you is less than ideal that means they are likely dealing with a lot of shit in their life, and so it's these people that actually need the most love. By reacting in the same way towards someone who is treating you poorly, you're more likely to keep getting the same behavior back. So, if your goal is to do away with that which you don't like, don't keep asking for the same experience through your equal reaction.

When we look at our relationships and the people we love through this lens, it becomes clear that the ONLY reaction we should ever have towards anyone is love. If someone's behavior is less than ideal towards us, meeting them at that same low vibrational place will only create more of that negative experience for both parties, when instead those are the people who need more love, and more love and more love.

The way you react determines what you're ready for. If you act low vibrationally the universe sees that you aren't ready for better. The way you respond has a direct effect on how much good you can attract into your reality. If you react the average way your experience will always be average.

Trust that in any given circumstance the universe puts you in to learn or help others learn, you have the tools you need within you and can react from this place of knowing.

If you feel someone is provoking you over and over again you should try to see it as a lesson, and when they poke you, love should come out, not anger, otherwise it shows you're just wearing love as a mask. When you really get it, and live it, love will always be the response. However, it's very important to remember again that in abusive situations, removing yourself is showing love also.

I know how hard this can be, I've had to live it in practice over and over again, from simple misunderstandings to assaults for things I had no control over, but I learned that I had control in how I reacted, and that always stayed with me. Be conscious instead of compulsive, and remember that badasses forgive, they don't fight.

At the end of the day, if you are mad at someone and harboring that anger, that is on you. You are choosing to live in that vibration, which, as we learned in Chapter 7, will only continue to invite more of the same.

This takes a lot of work and you have to remember what we talked about in Chapter 4 regarding dipping down into levels you have already passed. A person who is operating on a lower level will either consciously or subconsciously do something in an attempt to bring you down to their level via your reaction, then once you're on their level they will want to have their conversations. Identify this and don't engage. The outdated ego program wants to engage, but we upgraded, so keep that software up to date.

Going down levels lowers your frequency which will make you feel crazy. It's up to you to stay in a higher-level frequency as that will keep you stalwart and show people what to follow. Lead by this example. Don't dip.

When you think of engaging you must think of it as deep-sea diving. The more you go down, the more disoriented you'll become until you run out of oxygen, which will cause total confusion. The goal is to bring everyone up, and they will never come up by you going down.

Remember, nothing real can ever be threatened so don't react from fear. When you're poked, let love be the response. This does not mean no reaction. It means reacting with love. Never lose the ability to react. When we are mirrored by others, and by other things, we learn who we are. So be grateful for all experiences as gratitude will break the negative reinforcement.

When you are faced with anything, the only thing you should be paying attention to is your reaction. Is this who you are? If it feels right, go with it. If not, course correct and find your power in those moments.

LEVEL EIGHT

You are walking along the side of your new level, looking for a clue that may take you higher, but nothing is presenting itself today. So, you carry on and on, thinking how far you've come and how far you still have to go, with a feeling of excitement, rather than dread for the road ahead, the lessons to learn and the work to do as each lesson brings you closer to your goal.

You begin to wonder what you will do upon reaching the top, do I just climb back down? But you know deep down that pondering the pros and cons of the future is futile. If anything, it will all be bliss, which you'll likely experience once you've caught up with the intention you set at the outset.

Approaching a point of exhaustion under the hot sun and, seemingly without options, you hear a familiar buzzing sound, one you remember from summer days past, and you look around to find the source. It's behind you and then to the side, then behind you again, so you spin around to lock eyes with a curious hummingbird. It is effortlessly hovering at eye level, staring directly into your eye, and deeper.

It is said that hummingbirds are messengers from one dimension to another and that the frequency of sound that their wings generate in flight resonates very deeply with humans. You are instantly at peace and in awe of this small creature's ability to engender this feeling in you. The hummingbird has a dark green body, the color feels regal and its head is crowned with the most vibrant purple feathers you have ever seen, so much so that, when they catch the sunlight at just the right angle, it looks as if light is emanating from within the bird's head.

You revel in the fact that the hummingbird is returning your curiosity to such an extent, and you are content to let this stare down last as long as it can. What is the message this hummingbird has for me you wonder, and as you ponder this it begins to dart around you jovially until it seems to be beckoning you to follow it in the opposite direction you were initially walking. Of course, you follow.

This new companion is a welcome sight along your journey and you dutifully name the little adventurer Colibri, or hummingbird in Spanish. Colibri leads you up to the edge of the side of the Pyramid you have been climbing and turns the corner, at which you stop.

Somehow, this whole time you hadn't considered maneuvering onto another side to continue your journey. Colibri disappears around the corner as you stay put, for some reason unsure if you should follow. Then the tiny, magical bird with a heartbeat of over 1,200 beats per minute darts back around as if to say, 'are you coming?' And so, you snap out of doubt and follow.

You realize that you are communicating with this bird and something tells you that this is possible because of your raised vibration. Years of seeing hummingbirds before this have gone unrecognized, but now that your vibration is better aligned you can make out the messages.

As you begin to round the corner, it's almost as if you hadn't known another side existed. You become aware of this whole other aspect containing possibilities for ascension, but you were just so used to the side you were climbing you hadn't thought to check here.

Excitedly, you turn the corner and lose your footing on some sand, slipping towards the edge. You scramble to hold onto something but it is no use, you go over the edge and tumble down a level, hitting the stone hard.

Instantly your mind is full of thoughts of self-hatred, blame, judgement, such as 'how could I be so stupid?', and 'Why did I follow the hummingbird?'

But you check your reaction and almost as quickly as those thoughts entered your head, they are followed by thoughts of, 'What is the hummingbird trying to teach me?' Or, 'Why did it take me around the corner when I was doing fine on 'my side'? What can I learn from this?'

And with that, the energy dissipates and you are able to assess your situation. All in all, you realize that you could have easily watched your footing as you went, and you own that this was no one's fault but your own. Seeing as how you already figured out how to get up to the next level before, you have faith that it can be done again.

The sun is already setting at this point, so you look at it with gratitude that at least you'll be able to rest your head again tonight on a carpet, and, if all goes well, you'll wake up where you started the day today.

Little Colibri is nowhere in sight but you send your companion love and off you go to find the copper bucket which you locate easily because it is sitting right next to your sack, which means you'll also be getting dinner tonight. Suddenly you are grateful for the fall. Clearly the hummingbird knew you would need sustenance for the rest of your journey and so directed you back towards it.

You know that everything happens for a reason and so you flow with this reality. Who knows, maybe that fall down a level saved you a worse fall later down many more.

You eat some flatbread and a few dates, unroll the carpet, tie your sack around your back this time, and you lay your head down, telling yourself how much you love yourself, and your ego.

You look up at all the stars that are an extension of you, and with one last glance at the moon, that curiously seems as if it has been full for the past three nights, you close your eyes and drift off to sleep.

You won't always be able to control what happens in life, but you will always be able to control your reaction, and your reaction creates your reality.

CHAPTER 9

ENERGY

IT'S ALL-AROUND US AND IT DOESN'T LIE

By now, it's become quite widely understood that everything in our world and universe is made of energy, and everything is connected to everything else through energy fields. Quantum theory researchers discovered that, not only do particles consist of energy, but so also does the space between them. This is the so-called zero-point energy. Therefore, it is true to say:

Everything consists of energy, and everything is connected via energy.

So, as a vessel of energy, it is very important that you are aware of this fact and also aware of how to be in control of the energy that you are putting into the universe, because that energy will affect the energy of the things around you and between you and others. It follows that it will therefore affect how that energy comes back to you also. It's never been clearer that we are in control of our own experience down to the most finite level, which means that the onus is on us to make our energy amazing for ourselves and all those around us.

We've already spoken of unconditional love as an action, but as an energy it is the purest form of both you can display to yourself and others. You will notice that, on encountering people who really resonate at this frequency, it is either a joy to be around them, or we classify them as being out to lunch because it doesn't seem as though they are fazed by anything. Our discomfort in something like this only means that our ego feels threatened by it, so the energy adjustment needs to come from us.

The energy of love is the answer to everything. It's the highest vibrational power we possess, and the virtual fuel that will swiftly move us along our correct course, much as food and drink power our physical bodies. On that subject, what we put into our physical and mental tanks is the fuel that instructs our energy how to vibrate.

Without an optimal physical body, it will be hard to have an optimal energetic body and vice versa, so let's address this.

Food equals jet fuel.

It used to take us a month to cross the Atlantic by steam ship. Before this it would have taken as long as two months to make the voyage in a sail ship. Now we can do so in a mere number of hours, thanks to improved technology and fuel.

If we treat our bodies less than optimally by allowing addictions, vices and poor diet to be our fuel, it will take us much longer to reach our goals.

Conversely, if we treat our bodies like optimal machines, by providing ourselves with the best form of nutrients and abstaining from below-optimal mental and physical fuel sources, it would stand to reason that, in time, humans could become capable of time travel, much like how we have mastered the amount of time it takes us to cross the Atlantic. We are capable of compressing time with every positive choice we make.

We all know what it feels like to binge on junk food or TV. We know how we feel afterwards, what our motivation is like, what our output is like. All below optimal. Contrastingly, we all know what it feels like to be at the top of our game. Eating clean, exercising regularly, keeping our engines in tip-top shape. Like this, we are akin to the jet engine, and every decision we make that doesn't support this makes us less like the Concorde and more like a prop plane, then a steam ship, then a sailboat, followed by a sailboat without wind, then a canoe, then a canoe without oars, and so on.

If you are the captain of a large ship and you are aiming to bring your ship into port, then you need to start steering days in advance, and every little course correction impacts the accuracy and timing of getting your ship into port.

In the same way, our bodies are our vessels here on earth and every decision we make, everything we eat, drink, smoke, snort, believe, say, do, or feel is a course correction. Be it minor or major, it all plays a role in getting us to our final destinations.

If you were captaining this ship and you had the option to fill it with the best fuel, or some synthetic alternative, what would you choose? The answer is clear, yet the actions so often are not.

This is, yet again, because we react on impulse instead of with calculated mindful decision-making with our own betterment in mind.

Try this out for yourself for 90 days. Cut something out that you know slows your engine down, whether it's sugar or alcohol or television or shopping or sex or porn, or whatever it may be. Cut it out for 90 days and see how your course corrects.

The truth is, if you really feel like you can't live without it, it's always available to fall back on but, like I've already established in this book; the gratification that comes from being the boss of your life and optimizing your vessel will far outweigh the pleasure of something you know is making your goals further and further out of reach.

Be the jet engine.

LEVEL NINE

You awake with the sunlight but are afraid to open your eyes. You're filled with dread that maybe that carpet trick was a one-time thing. So, you lie there unsure of what to do, knowing full well that nothing will change the reality you are already in except your reaction to it, so you willingly open your eyes and look towards the wall. No copper bucket. So far so good. You look over the edge. Copper bucket! And this time your sack is tied firmly to your back! You kiss the carpet, roll it up and drop it down back into its vessel with stunning accuracy. Thanks to that fall, you're better off than you were yesterday! Gratitude!

And off you go in search of Colibri, this time of course, minding your footing as you round the corner because we only need to learn a lesson once, as our gut reminds us.

Upon rounding the corner, the vista that opens up on this side is never ending. Such an expanse, unlike any you have ever seen. You are mesmerized by the sheer vastness of this magnificent world and all the bounty she has to offer us.

A familiar buzzing materializes overhead. Colibri! Good morning, you beautiful, majestic bird! The little bird tilts her head just a bit, as if she's saying, nice to see you too. Watch your step this time! You follow Colibri, her purple feathers lighting the way as they come into contact with the sunlight. You see a sloping rock looming ahead. On reaching it, you realize it is the top of a doorway or support system of some sort which began a level or two below, but at this level will provide you swift and easy access up to the next. Colibri disappears under the awning of the doorway, which is not visible to you, and so you conclude that your tiny but mighty bird has taken you as far as she will and has now retreated home.

You give thanks and place your foot on the stone just as Colibri comes back into sight with three baby hummingbirds that must have just learned to fly that very morning. Such a sight you have never seen. Tiny hummingbird chicks, taking their first flight, something you might have missed had you not fallen down a level the day before.

Such gratitude you feel for the fall, the journey, and Colibri with these young hummingbirds, the sound of all of their wings in unison sending a clear message of love and the highest of vibrational energy, which is all the fuel you need to ascend to the next level, and so you do, with ease.

Cultivate a habit of turning within before engaging without and remember that energy doesn't lie.

CHAPTER 10

VIBRATION

IN PRACTICE

Now that we understand what energy is, it's time to talk about the output of our energy, which is in short, our vibration.

You know how when you meet someone and you say that their vibe was off, or it felt weird? That isn't you misinterpreting a scenario, you were actually feeling the energetic vibration of the situation or person and reacting to it with yours. Remember how we talked about the scientific fact of the space between things containing energy in the last chapter? Feeling a vibe is an example of that.

Similarly, do you know that feeling when you think someone's looking at you and you turn around and see in fact that someone is? Energy casts a feeling.

This is also why relationships break apart. Sometimes people meet, both having been at the same vibration, but over time one of them will either go higher or lower, meaning that the other person's vibration no longer matches. In this case the pair experience friction and naturally move away from one another. Problems arise when one or the other tries to get the other person to either come up or down to their new level. You cannot force someone onto your level no matter how honorable your intentions, it won't happen. What you can do, the only thing you can, is to honor your energy and your vibration and lead by example.

Then, and only then, can we set an energetic path for others to follow. If we understood this and realized that the only focus should be continuing to change ourselves or continuing to honor our high vibrations, it would save us so much grief. Instead, we so often try to discuss why this person should do this or do that, which only brings both of our vibratory frequencies down. It's a lose-lose for everyone. We have one job, and that job is to keep our own vibration high.

When we keep our vibration high, we invite high vibrational people and experiences to join us along our journey. When our vibe is low we invite low vibrational experiences and people into our journey. This is why it is so important to make your vibrational output a priority in your life as it sets the tone for all your experiences. You cannot rely on anyone else or any other thing to raise your vibe as you have to do it yourself. Meet people where they are, show love, raise the vibration and lead by healing yourself first.

You need to find what it is that raises your vibration and you need to make it a consistent part of your life, and a priority.

I love the word selfish, because it fascinates me how it has negative connotations. In fact, being selfish towards enhancing your vibration is the most unselfish thing you can do for yourself and everyone in your life. If you put anything but your vibe first then everything including your vibe suffers and that, is selfish. Unfortunately, somehow the meaning of the word has been misinterpreted and we were left with the idea that being selfless was the admirable choice. The truth is, being selfish in the way this book proposes, is selfless.

So, what can we do to raise our vibe? It will be different for each of us, but I find that there are practices that have been in place for thousands of years for a reason. Meditation, breath-work and grounding are at the top of that list.

In addition, music, because it is easily accessible and for the most part, we all love it in one form or another. On the subject of musical form I could write a whole chapter, but again, I will keep it brief. Music is the easiest way to regulate your vibration but choose wisely. What happens when you listen to aggravating music? You feel aggravated. What happens when you listen to the sound of a singing bowl? Relaxation. This isn't about musical preferences, it's about the energetic make-up of our biological bodies. We organically resonate with certain sounds and frequencies and not with others.

Ancient instruments such as Tibetan bowls, Pythagoras' monochord, ancient flutes, have all been coincidentally found to use 432Hz as their base pitch. Mozart and Verdi used 432Hz for all their music. Hertz is a modern term coined in 1930, but before that, musicians referred to Cycles Per Second. The first time Cycles Per Second could be accurately measured was in 1834, and there are a lot of theories surrounding this specific frequency but, from experience, I know that it resonates well with the human body. This is why so many sleep apps use classical music in their programming.

Whatever your choice, find what causes you to feel constantly high vibrational, and make it a part of your daily routine, making sure you aren't using a vice to do so. An easy way to tell is whether, when you are done interacting, you feel expansive or restricted? Then eliminate or re-engage on this basis. Put your vibration first and foremost above any other obligation as it will influence anything and everything you do during the day.

Of course, it's important to remove yourself from situations where there is a big energy imbalance, but I challenge you to raise your vibration and put it to good use too by raising the collective energy and experience for all. Never doubt the power you possess. This isn't just to benefit the vibe at a dinner party, but your health relies on it too.

In 2019 I was hospitalized with an infection that doctors couldn't identify, and thus misdiagnosed a few times over the course of a week, as it got worse and worse. I forgot my practices amidst the pain and continued to look to the doctors for help. It wasn't until the last trip to the Emergency Room, in total despair, that I was sitting on a gurney in the hallway, clutching myself in pain when I had a thought. Your vibe is really, really low right now, no wonder your body can't heal.

So, what do I do now, I thought to myself? Meditate. Something I had forgotten to do since the pain had started.

I pulled a blanket over my head and began to meditate. At the end of 20 minutes I sat upright at the end of the bed, took a deep breath, the first one in almost two weeks and decided to myself that I would heal. I was discharged from the hospital, that afternoon, went home and fell asleep for the first time in three days. After that, I began healing and within a week was back to normal.

Unbeknownst to myself I had somehow taken a photo of myself with my phone as I sat at the edge of the hospital bed. When I happened upon it a few days later, I saw that the picture depicted me with a strong gold aura that I believe I had activated in the meditation and the camera somehow captured. I know how that sounds, but the photo speaks for itself.

As we are made of energy, naturally it makes sense to use energy to heal ourselves and one another. This is why it is so important to try to not to be stressed alongside illness. I know it sounds hard, but the most important thing you can possibly do when sick, is to find stillness in something like meditation to bring your stress down and your vibration up.

Do not give your energy over to the shadows of worry. You're doing double work because the energy of worry drains you and pollutes your environment.

The pure energy of a high vibration is all the fuel you need, and you can tap into it any time. The more you keep your vibe high the more accessible it will always be.

Meditate, dance, hike, sing, laugh, look at hummingbirds, kiss, make love. Whatever it takes to keep that vibe high.

LEVEL TEN

Colibri's baby hummingbirds accompany you all the way up the slanted rock to the next level of the Pyramid. You can't help but feel the vibration these tiny birds are giving off. They are reminders that energy is all around us and especially now in the spaces in-between their fluttering wings and me, you think to yourself.

You take them in one last time as they hover happily around you, experiencing their first flight. Then one by one, they flutter effortlessly back down to where their nest must be. The sound of their baby wings is a sound you won't ever forget.

You turn and find yourself staring at the base of the capstone of the Pyramid. It looks close enough to touch. Somehow you hadn't realized you were this close to the top, but you're not there yet.

You look up. The next portion looks challenging. The rock seems to jut out in an insurmountable way due to the stones having crumbled away from the lower portion that you had been climbing. Too bad you can't get an army of little hummingbirds to carry you up.

With this thought you're reminded of a tale you heard of the Aztecs and how they had an elite sect of warriors known as hummingbird warriors, who were recognized as being evolved and privileged as they would reincarnate as warriors again and again, which was a great honor.

The Aztecs believed that hummingbirds carried messages from one realm to another and, upon witnessing these powerful baby hummingbirds, you knew this to be true. For this reason you also accepted what felt like a charge from Colibri and her babies for you to step into your role as a hummingbird warrior, a master of self and warrior of light who would again and again reincarnate to bring this light to the world and all those with whom you come into contact.

Your chest swells with pride and your stance strikes firm on this tenth ledge of the Pyramid. There's one more level to go and then you're at the top. The wind starts to blow uncontrollably as you step into this role, as if it had been waiting for you to do so since the day of your birth, but knowing full well you would do so in your own time. For as we know, everything in our lives happens in good time.

The swelling wind blows stronger and stronger as you open your arms to it. It picks you up and carries you with the grace and efficiency of a hummingbird to the eleventh level of the Pyramid. There is one more lesson to learn, and then, you'll be at the top.

Stop looking for the light. Become it. All we can do is be a consistent source of light so that others can themselves start to glow.

CHAPTER 11

ATTRACTION

VISUALIZATION

So here we are, we've made it to the penultimate level of the Pyramid. So, what do we need to know now?

Well, first of all, that this moment is inevitable. And so is this one, and this one, and you already didn't fuck any of this up.

So far, we have learned a few important truths.

- We know that life is for enjoyment. But do we also know that it is for enjoyment at all times? Not just the highs of distraction followed by the lows in between. If it's not consistent and the contrast positive, it doesn't count.
- So, in knowing all that we do, what can we do to make each moment the best it can be? We have established that happiness is not an occasion, but rather a constant state of existence through our perception, and one we are in control of at all times, because we know that cause and effect both reside within us.

- We know we are the only ones in control of our own lives. We understand that, if we blame external forces, then we are giving our power over to those things, and therefore proclaiming that we have no control over our own lives.
- We know that we shape our existence through our reactions and by making friends with our ego.
- We can quiet the mind, align the gut, listen to our body, and thus we can let things flow.
- We are lovingly self-disciplined and we make sure we are treating our physical vessel like the optimal machine it is.

From here, all that is left to do is take all these inherent strengths and manifest our ultimate reality by remembering something quite simple.

A seed, when planted and nurtured with water, has all of the information within it to become whatever plant it set out to be when the seed was created. You are a seed that has all of the information inside of you already, you just have to remember it, and once you do, you will be able to stop blocking your own path.

We have learned that we do not need to suffer things which do not yet exist, however most of the time the internal monologue that runs in our head is making us do just that. We speculate, we worry, we plan, we project. All with the best of intentions of course, but at the end of the day it's all for naught.

We have come to think it normal to ponder worst-case scenarios and we are told, even from our earliest schooldays that it is unhealthy to daydream. Best to get your head out of the clouds and keep your feet on the ground.

Well, if your thoughts create your reality then why aren't we constantly thinking the best thoughts all the time, no matter how ridiculous we ourselves might think said thoughts are?

If speculation and worry are lowering your vibration, then, based on what we have already learned, we know we cannot engage in thoughts like this. So, if daydreaming about your dream job, or partner, or life, or whatever, raises your vibration, then start daydreaming! Fill your day with the happiest thoughts that lift you off the ground and send your vibration out into the universe clearly indicating what you are asking, and ready, for.

When we worry, we send that vibration out into the world and, in return, we get experiences that match that frequency.

When we dream of achieving our goals then our brains record these wins and give us the feeling of having achieved them, aligning us with that experience and laying the foundation for taking the next steps towards creating them in 3D.

A fascinating part of the brain is known as the Reticular Activating System (RAS) and it, conveniently, does not know the difference between what is actually happening to us and what we tell it has happened to us. So, when we say demeaning things to ourselves, they are recorded as fact.

When we say empowering and delightful things to ourselves, they too are recorded as fact.

The saying that you create your own reality is in evidence here as your thoughts actually drive this wonderful part of our brains.

Your Reticular Activating System takes what you focus on and creates a filter for it through your conscious and subconscious minds. It then spends its time going through the data it has received (for example, what you have experienced that day), highlighting the relevant events that confirm what is most important to you. It then decides to prioritize based on what you are thinking, taking instruction from your conscious mind, and passing it on to your subconscious mind.

You know how you can always hear your name when it's said in a crowd? That's an example of your RAS highlighting what it believes to be important to you. So, if you take control of this system and by instructing it what is important to focus on, it will start highlighting parts of your day to bring you closer to your goals.

For example, setting positive intent around a particular goal or interest, and declaring that goal or interest to yourself, is a way for you to get this system to make it a reality.

According to the Merriam-Webster Dictionary, the word intent is derived from the word intend, which means to direct the mind and proceed on course towards a goal. The origin of 'intent' is the Latin verb *intendere*, which means to stretch towards.

It's quite straightforward. Focus on bad things and you will invite those things into your life. Focus on good things and you will invite those things into your life because you are unknowingly telling your RAS to seek them out. This is the enacted example of the change of filter conversation we were having earlier in this book. The problem is that we're setting it up to point out what we don't like most of the time. This part of our brain makes sure that whatever you are thinking about will seep down into your subconscious mind only to reappear at a future time to confirm itself. For example, if you think you are terrible at public speaking, as I did, then you will likely continue to have a terrible time when you have to stand up and give a speech.

The more you think about it, the more you manifest it.

Here's an example of how I make the RAS work for me. I do public speaking occasionally for my brand and I have a nervous stutter that's been following me around since I was a kid. I get nervous, then I stutter. So, it's understandable that when it comes to my turn to speak in front of a room of 100 people, I stammer up. That is, until I learned about the Reticular Activating System.

When I feel the nerves coming on and don't know where to put them, I say to myself, 'I'm not nervous to speak, these feelings of anxiety are actually excitement. I can't wait to speak to this crowd and I intend to do an excellent job.' The RAS records the physical feelings of anxiety instead as excitement, and when the microphone is passed to me, I nail it, every time.

What I notice happening when I'm telling myself that my nerves are not anxiety but excitement, is that I actually switch into believing that statement. I become aware that whether I say I can, or whether I say I can't, I'm speaking the truth.

I set the intent, which sends my Reticular Activating System a message that I am expecting this event to happen just as I say it should. As you can see, this practice is a powerful way of directing your energy towards your future goal.

Taking it a step farther, and if you have the time, actually picture having just spoken to the crowd and having done an excellent job at it. It's like reverse manifestation, imagining that what you want to happen has already happened, and reflecting positively on the outcome of that success.

Manifestation through reverse creative visualization requires focusing on the what without the how and then reciting it to yourself as if it already happened. This takes practice and repetition but it feels great once you get the hang of it. If you want your muscles to grow you have to go to the gym and work on them, this same dedication applies here.

If you find you are focusing on the negative by default, which can happen quite often, as we know, simply let go of the incorrect version of your manifestation. We just have to look at it and say 'incorrect version'. If we focus on the negative version we give it reality and solidify it further. Recognize it, release it, and allow the universe to sweep it away as the wind does with clouds, revealing sunshine.

This becomes very powerful if put into practice when you are with others. By setting your intention beforehand to have a loving and wonderful time with those you plan to spend time with, your RAS will continue to illuminate things during your time together that confirm this experience. By making the loving examples of your time together more noticeable, your reactions will be geared towards the things that your RAS highlights, and so by setting your intent and having your RAS go to bat for you by highlighting your positive intentions, you're doing good for your own experience, and the experience of those around you.

We don't have to save this for things like public speaking. We can be wallowing in heartbreak but tell ourselves, 'I love how this experience has shaped me into a strong, confident and unconditionally loving person,' reflecting back on the heartbreak from a place of calm love, and implementing a thought of pleasure to break you out of a negative thought pattern.

A thought of pleasure requires thinking of something, anything, that would make you extremely happy and that you can recall with ease. Spend some time on this, and when you have it, write it down and call it up whenever you need to. You can change this thought at any time but I find it useful to hone in on one specific thought of pleasure, whatever it may be, so that it is easy for you to call it up whenever you need it to flip a negative thought pattern.

An example of something I like to call up is sitting around a big brunch table with my entire family and extended family, fresh white roses on the table, a plentiful spread of food, laughter, love and excellent coffee.

Thoughts of pleasure alter low vibrational feelings into high vibrational ones instantly, and as we now know, our brain records the experience for us as reality, so why not step into brunch throughout the day as I often do. It's a lovely way to stop and smell the roses.

The truth is that all realities are happening concurrently, and we have the power to align ourselves with the one that pleases us the most at any time, we just have to tell our minds to take the best version of ourselves there in 5D so that we can experience it here in 3D.

Living like this keeps the eye of your heart open and allows you to write your own story, not live it as if it were already written based on your past and present.

LEVEL ELEVEN

You stand at the highest level of the Pyramid. All that remains is to ascend to the very top, on which there is a small flat area you can make out and from there, you would likely see the entire world.

You look behind you and realize that the height to which you have climbed is truly monumental and you think to yourself how impressive it is that you came this far despite how afraid you are of heights. This thought instantly makes you begin to doubt your ability to go any higher.

You shake your head, and tell yourself that in fact you love heights, because from the highest height you can see the farthest, and you want to see everything.

You put down your sack and your water bottle, ridding yourself of any loose items. With all the strength in your incredible body you crouch down and then leap up and grasp the base of the capstone, hanging off of it for a moment before you slip off. Again. Again. Again. Each time looking down and becoming wearier of trying again. 'I love heights' you repeat to yourself.

You remove your boots and try again, but this time when your hands grasp the edge, your feet are able to brace your position and you know you'll make it up with your bare hands and bare feet, bare as the day you were born. It takes small, careful movements, but the whole time you repeat to yourself what an excellent and fearless climber you are, so that each maneuver feels more natural than the one that preceded it. You are noticing that your reality is unfolding in front of you as you are saying it will.

You give a final push using equal strength with all four limbs and you heave yourself up and over and directly onto the top of the Pyramid.

Panting, with sand on your face, you stand.

Directly in front of you, the sun is setting yet again. You turn to see the moon rising directly behind you. The entire world is visible now. Your perspective is clear and your heart open, making your sense of self love radiate from within with an intensity to match the sun's rays.

The air is calm and still and you sense motion all around you. At first you can't make out what it is but then it becomes clear that countless butterflies of all shapes, sizes and colors are dancing around the summit of the Pyramid, as they do most days, but today, they dance around you. The spectacle reminds you of their beautiful ability to change from a caterpillar to this magnificent winged creature you see before you at dusk.

You turn again and again, watching the butterflies dance in the setting sunlight by themselves and in occasional groups of two and three and four, reminding you of the importance of flying solo but also of sharing this journey of life with those you love, whether for a short time or a long time, without any attachment or expectations. To simply shine and fly in your purest form the way these butterflies do.

This understanding is what you strove to achieve.

As the sun shines its last light, the butterflies retreat to their nighttime retreats, to join the hummingbirds in the realm of magic and infinite possibilities, so that they can come back to this dimension tomorrow and share with us all they have learned from that realm.

You turn to face the moon, your constant and most trusted advisor. Tonight, it is at its fullest, and when it is most full, it has the most important lessons to relay. You watch the moon's silver light cover the land and you follow its glow until it bathes your bare hands and feet. Gazing now at your feet, you see something glistening between them, stuck directly in the center of the top of the Pyramid.

You bend down to retrieve it and, with a bit of effort you finally manage to loosen the object and take it out. Holding it up to the moonlight you recognize it instantly as a piece of labradorite. You have heard that, once this stone finds you, it awakens your innate magical powers and psychic abilities, clearing the aura of negative energies, transforming intuition into intellectual thoughts, and directs you to your life's purpose, making you the master of your vessel.

You watch the stone glisten in the moon's full glow and know that tonight of all nights is when it recharges the energy it expended over the last month. So, as you lie down, you place the labradorite next to you to make sure you both absorb as much moonlight as you can tonight, knowing that the light of the full moon will equip you to face the journey down the Pyramid, back to your life in the town, so you can begin leading by example by sharing all that you have learned on this journey.

Your stone of labradorite will always be on your person from this day forward, to provide protection and guidance as you continue along this path and show others the way. A way which will be well-lit for you by the stone, and well-lit for others by your inner light, which you'll keep shining as brightly as the full moon above, as you drift off to sleep.

Remember, it's always ok in the end and if it's not ok, it's not the end.

The more you think about it, the more you manifest it.

V, IV, III, II, I

Greater than imagined.

ABOUT THE AUTHOR

Adam Taubenfligel was born in Canada and now resides in California with his dog, Frenchie. He is Creative Director and Sustainability Lead at Triarchy Denim (@triarchy), where his mission is to eliminate the unnecessary use of water and chemicals in denim production. Through this journey it became apparent that intention and mindfulness are the key to achieving sustainable manufacturing practices and responsible consumer habits, and so he believes in the importance of employing intention and mindfulness in all that we do. His first book, "Setting An Intention: 11 Brief Lessons On Achieving Your Greater Good", is a handbook on doing just that.

Printed in Great Britain
by Amazon

25154361R00086